THE ESSENTIAL

CHICKEN

COOKBOOK

THE ESSENTIAL CHICKEN COOKBOOK

EXCITING NEW WAYS WITH A CLASSIC INGREDIENT

Linda Fraser

SWEET WATER PRESS

First published in 1998 by Sweetwater Press
by arrangement with Anness Publishing Limited

Produced by Anness Publishing Limited
Hermes House
88–89 Blackfriars Road
London SE1 8HA

ISBN 1-58173-023-3

Publisher: Joanna Lorenz
Cookery Editors: Rosemary Wilkinson, Linda Doeser
Designers: Bill Mason, Siân Keogh
Illustrator: Anna Koska

Front Cover: Lisa Tai, Designer; Thomas Odulate, Photographer;
Helen Trent, Stylist; Lucy McKelvie, Home Economist

Recipes: Catherine Atkinson, Alex Barker, Ruby Le Bois, Carla Capalbo, Maxine Clark, Andi Clevely,
Christine France, Carole Handslip, Sarah Gates, Shirley Gill, Norma MacMillan, Sue Maggs, Katherine
Richmond, Jenny Stacey, Liz Trigg, Hilaire Walden, Laura Washburn, Steven Wheeler
Photographers: Karl Adamson, Edward Allwright, Steve Baxter, James Duncan, John Freeman,
Michelle Garrett, Amanda Heywood, Don Last
Food for Photography: Marilyn Forbes, Carole Handslip, Jane Harsthorn, Cara Hobday, Beverly LeBlanc,
Wendy Lee, Lucy McKelvie, Jenny Shapter, Elizabeth Silver, Jane Stevenson,
Liz Trigg, Elizabeth Wolf-Cohen

Previously published as part of a larger compendium: *Best-Ever Chicken*

Printed in Hong Kong/China

1 3 5 7 9 10 8 6 4 2

NOTE
Standard spoon and cup measurements are level.

Contents

Introduction

Chicken is one of the most astonishingly versatile ingredients in any kitchen, anywhere in the world. Delicious, nutritious, economical, and with a distinctive flavor of its own, it combines superbly with all kinds of other ingredients—from herbs and spices to vegetables and pasta, and from cream and yogurt to soy and chili sauces. You can roast, casserole, or pot roast the whole bird or cook separate portions, from drumsticks and wings, to boneless breasts and other cuts, as well as preparing made-in-minutes dishes from sliced, chopped, or ground breast and thigh.

This book is crammed with mouthwatering ways of preparing chicken, some familiar and others rather more unusual. It is divided into six chapters. Soups & Appetizers offers a collection of warming, filling broths, as well as lighter first courses. Meals in Minutes includes delicious quick and easy recipes to provide interesting, filling, and tasty meals for the family throughout the year. Casseroles and Bakes offers a choice of traditional "winter warmers," while Salads, Barbecues & Grills is packed full of recipes just right for warm summer evenings. Roasts & Pies offers both traditional and new ways with chicken, while Hot & Spicy provides a fiery finale!

A useful introductory section offers guidance on choosing whole birds and individual cuts of chicken, step-by-step instructions on trussing, advice on roasting, a selection of scrumptious stuffings, and hints on making that invaluable standby, chicken stock.

Chicken is easy to prepare and cook, whether fresh or frozen, whole or portioned. Make sure that frozen chicken, especially when still on the bone, is completely thawed before you start to prepare it and that all chicken is thoroughly cooked before you serve it.

Choosing a Chicken

A fresh chicken should have a plump breast and the skin should be creamy in color. The tip of the breast bone should be pliable.

A bird's dressed weight is taken after plucking and drawing and may include the giblets (neck, gizzard, heart and liver). A frozen chicken must be thawed slowly in the fridge or a cool room. Never put it in hot water, as this will toughen the flesh and is dangerous as it allows bacteria to multiply.

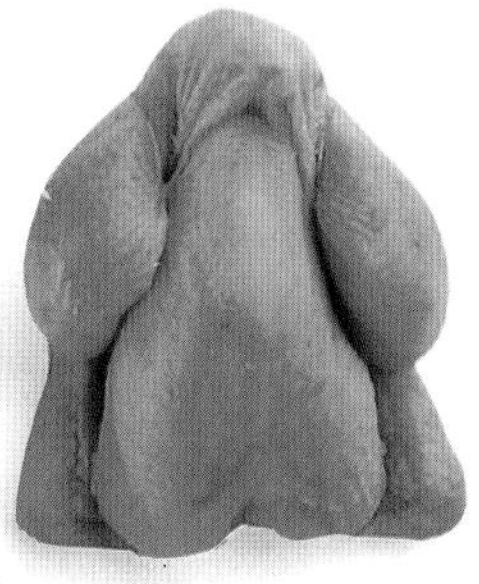

Rock Cornish hens
These are four to six weeks old and weigh $1\text{–}1^{1}/_{4}$ pounds. One is enough for one person.

Broiling chickens
These are eight to ten weeks old and weigh $1^{3}/_{4}\text{–}2$ pounds. One will serve two people. Poussins are best roasted, broiled or pot-roasted.

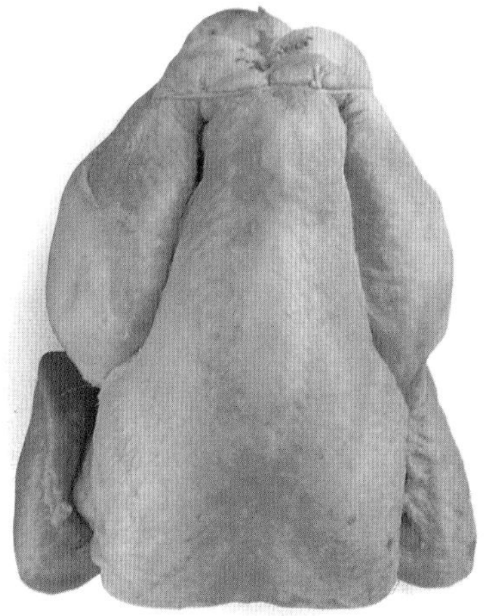

Roasters
These birds are about six to twelve months old and weigh 3–6 pounds. One will feed a family.

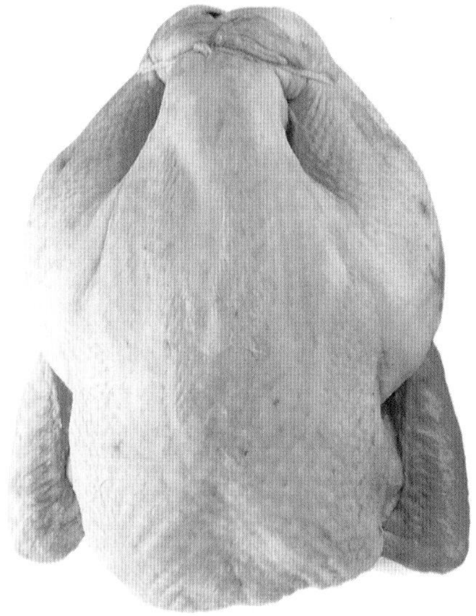

Boiling fowl
These are about twelve months old and over and weigh between 4–6 pounds. They require long, slow cooking, around 2–3 hours, to make them tender.

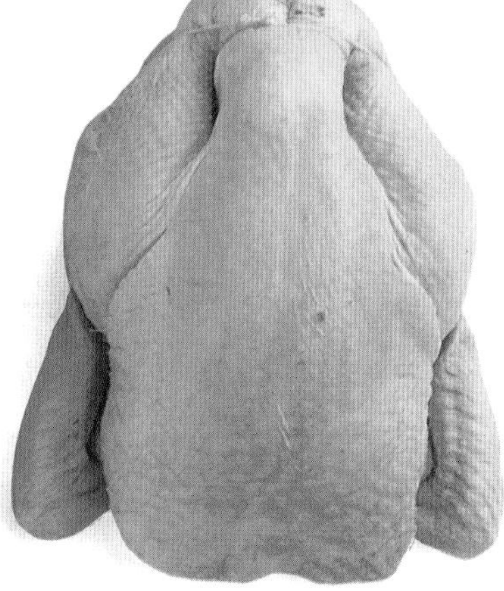

Corn-fed chickens
These are free-range birds, and are generally more expensive. They usually weigh $2^{1}/_{2}\text{–}3$ pounds.

Frying chickens
These birds are about three months old and weigh 2–3 pounds. One will serve three to four people.

Cuts of Chicken

Chicken pieces are available pre-packaged in various forms. If you do not want to buy a whole bird, you can make your choice from the many cuts on the market.

Some cooking methods are especially suited to specific cuts of poultry.

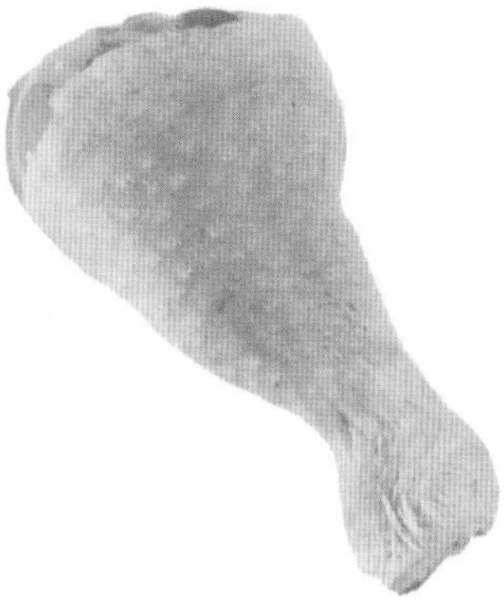

Drumstick
The drumstick is a firm favorite for barbecuing or frying, either in batter or rolled in breadcrumbs.

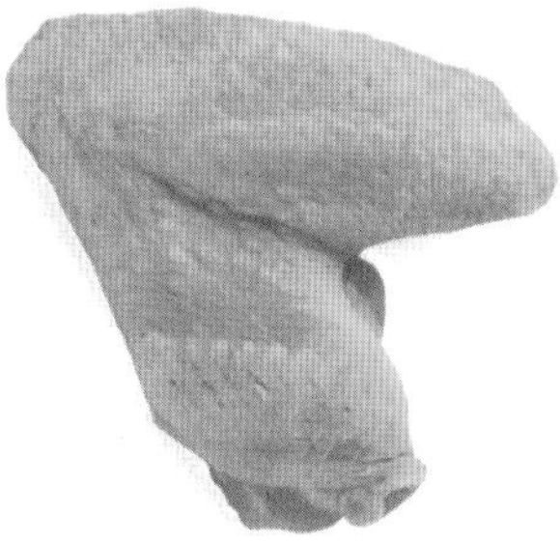

Wing
The wing does not supply much meat, and is often barbecued or fried.

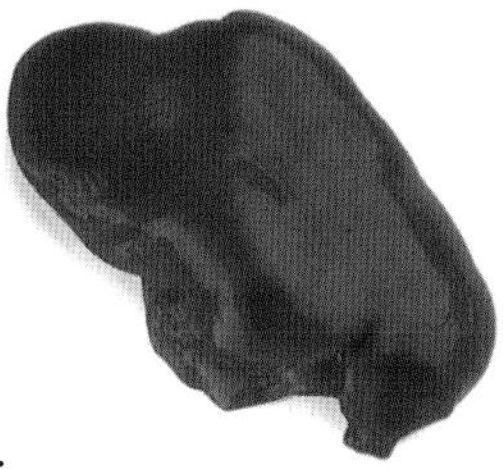

Liver
This makes a wonderful addition to pâtés or to salads.

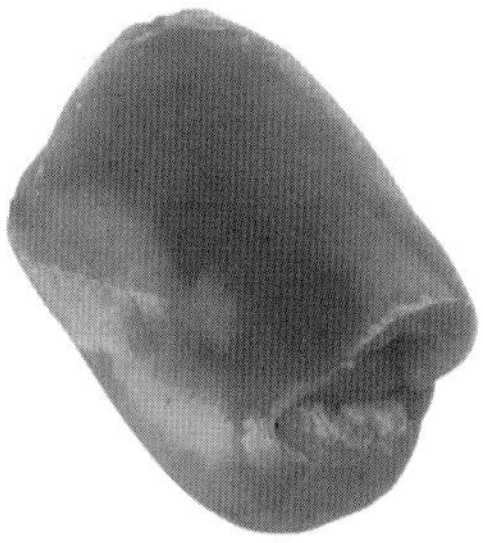

Skinless boneless thigh
This makes tasks such as stuffing and rolling much quicker, as it is already skinned and dis-jointed.

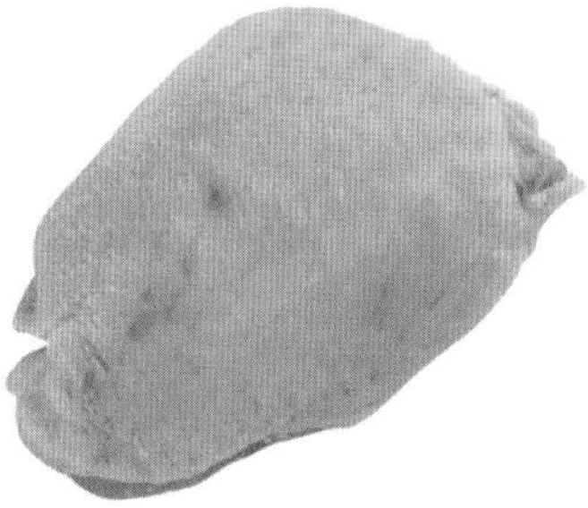

Thigh
The thigh is suitable for casseroling and other slow-cooking methods.

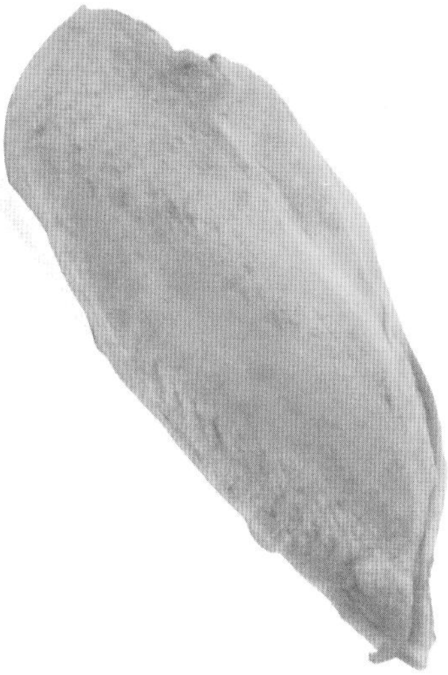

Breast
The tender white meat can be simply cooked in butter, or can be stuffed for extra flavor.

Ground chicken
This is not as strongly flavored as, say, ground beef, but it may be used as a substitute in some recipes.

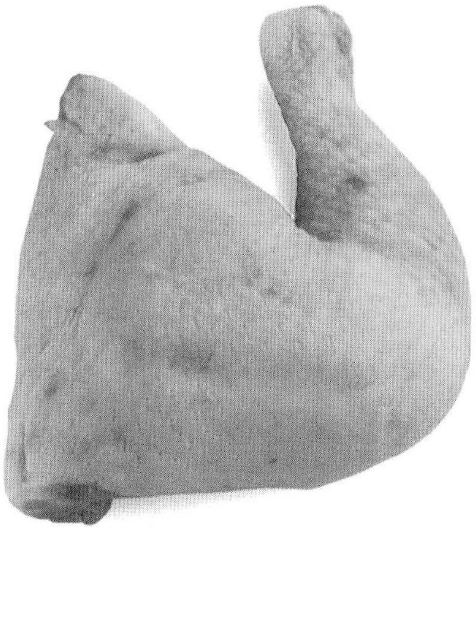

Leg
This comprises the drumstick and thigh. Large pieces with bones, such as this, are suitable for slow-cooking, such as casseroling or poaching.

Trussing Poultry

Trussing holds a bird together during cooking so that it keeps a neat, attractive shape. If the bird is stuffed, trussing prevents the stuffing from falling out. You can truss with strong string or poultry skewers.

An alternative to the method shown here is to use a long trussing needle and fine cotton string: make two passes, in alternate directions, through the body at the open end, from wing to wing, and tie. Then pass the needle through the pope's nose and tie the string around the ends of the drumsticks.

Remove trussing before serving.

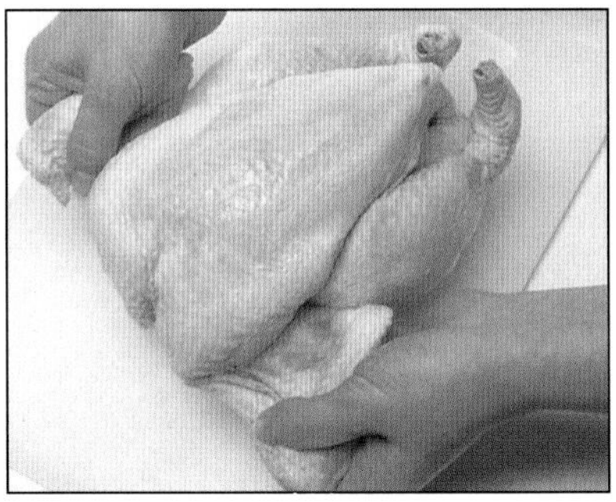

1 For an unstuffed bird: set it breast down and pull the neck skin over the neck opening. Turn the bird breast up and fold the wing tips back, over the skin, to secure behind the shoulders.

2 Press the legs down firmly and into the breast. If there is a band of skin across the pope's nose, fold back the ends of the drumsticks and tuck them under the skin.

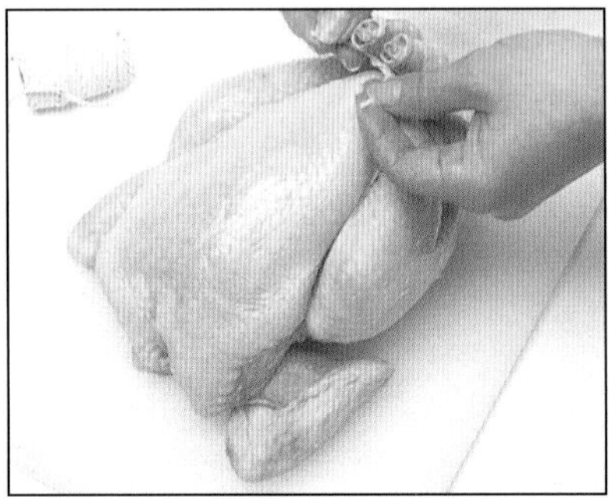

3 Otherwise, cross the knuckle ends of the drumsticks or bring them tightly together. Loop a length of string several times around the drumstick ends, tie a knot and trim off excess string.

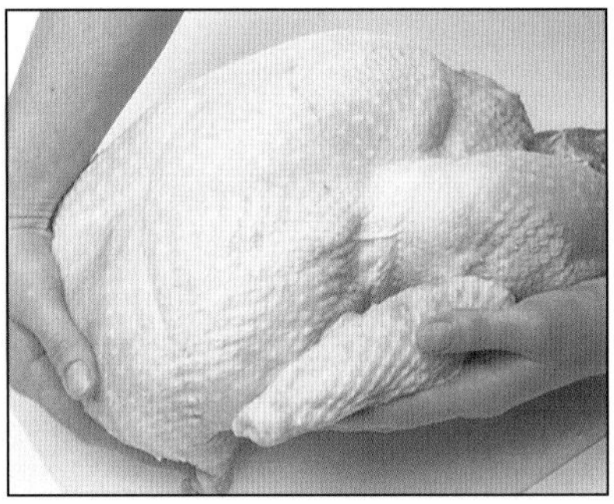

4 For a stuffed bird: fold the wing tips back as above. After stuffing the neck end, fold the flap of skin over the opening and secure it with a skewer, then fold over the wing tips.

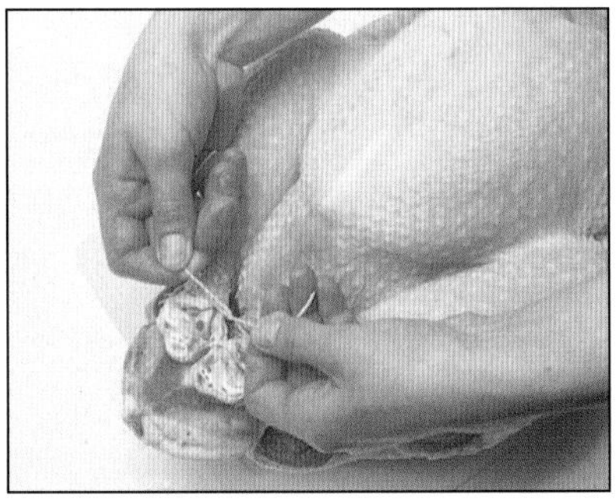

5 Put any stuffing or flavorings (herbs, lemon halves, apple quarters and so on) in the body cavity, then secure the ends of the drumsticks as above, tying in the pope's nose, too.

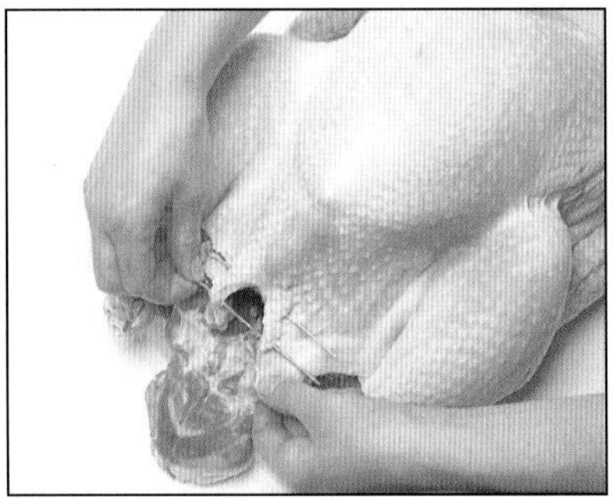

6 Or, the cavity opening can be closed with skewers: insert two or more skewers across the opening, threading them through the skin several times.

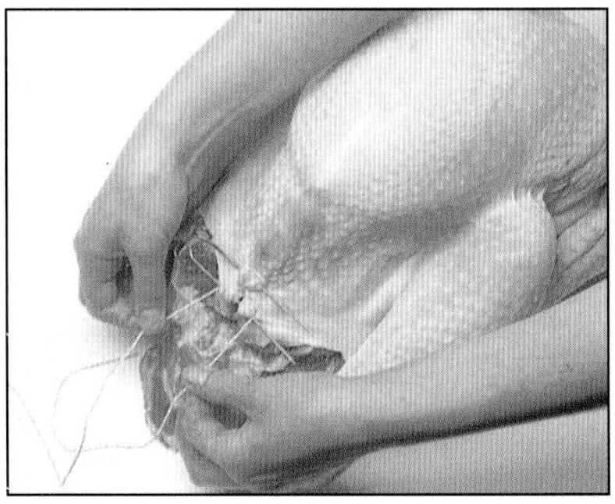

7 Lace the skewers together with string. Tie the drumsticks together over the skewers.

STUFFING TIPS

Only use stuffing that is cool, not hot or chilled. Pack it loosely in the bird and cook any leftovers separately. Stuff poultry just before cooking. Do not stuff the body cavity of a large bird because this could inhibit heat penetration, and thus harmful bacteria may not be destroyed.

Roasting Poultry

Where would family gatherings be without the time-honored roast bird? Beyond the favorite chicken, all types of poultry can be roasted – from Rock Cornish hens to large turkeys. However, older, tougher birds are better pot-roasted.

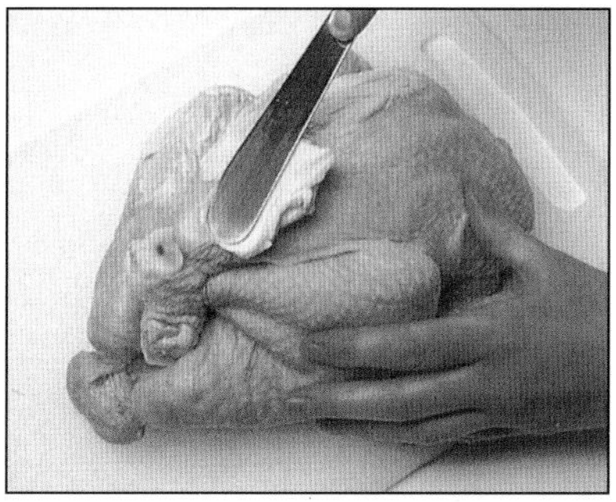

1 Wipe the bird inside and out with damp paper towels, stuff, if desired and truss it. Spread the breast of chicken with soft butter or oil; bard a lean game bird; prick the skin of duck or goose.

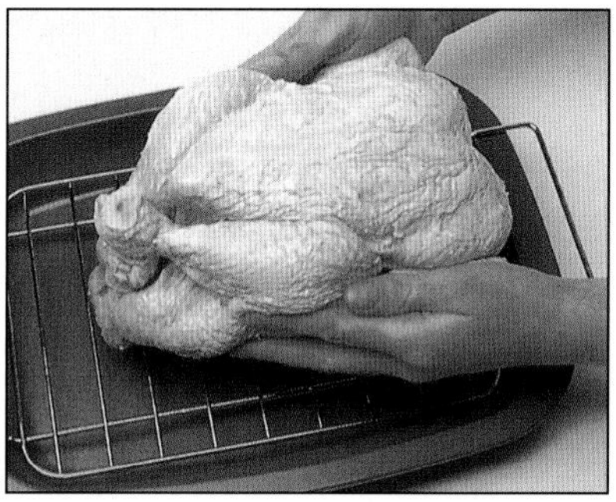

2 Set the bird breast up on a rack in a small roasting pan or shallow baking dish. If you are roasting a lean game bird, set the bird in the pan breast down.

3 Roast the bird, basting every 10 minutes after the first 30 minutes with the juices and fat in the pan. If browning too quickly, cover with foil.

4 Put the bird on a carving board and let it rest for at least 15 minutes before serving. Meanwhile make a simple sauce or gravy with the juices in the pan.

SIMPLE ROAST CHICKEN

Squeeze the juice from a halved lemon over a 3–3 1/2-pound chicken, then push the lemon halves into the body cavity. Smear 1 tablespoon softened butter over the breast. Roast in a 375°F oven for about 1 1/4 hours. Skim all fat from the roasting juices, then add 1/2 cup water and bring to a boil, stirring well to mix in the browned bits. Season with salt and pepper, and serve this sauce with the chicken. Serves 4.

ROASTING TIMES FOR POULTRY

Note: Cooking times given here are for unstuffed birds. For stuffed birds, add 20 minutes to the total roasting time.

Rock Cornish Hen	1–1 1/2 pounds	1–1 1/4 hours at 350°F
Chicken	2 1/2–3 pounds	1–1 1/4 hours at 375°F
	3 1/2–4 pounds	1 1/4–2 hours at 375°F
	4 1/2–5 pounds	1 1/2–2 hours at 375°F
	5–6 pounds	1 3/4–2 1/2 hours at 375°F
Duck	3–5 pounds	1 3/4–2 1/4 hours at 400°F
Goose	8–10 pounds	2 1/2–3 hours at 350°F
	10–12 pounds	3–3 1/2 hours at 350°F
Turkey	6–8 pounds	3–3 1/2 hours at 325°F
(whole bird)	8–12 pounds	3–4 hours at 325°F
	12–16 pounds	4–5 hours at 325°F
Turkey	4–6 pounds	1 1/2–2 1/4 hours at 325°F
(whole breast)	6–8 pounds	2 1/4–3 1/4 hours at 325°F

PROTECT & FLAVOR

Before roasting, loosen the skin on the breast by gently easing it away from the flesh with your fingers. Press in softened butter – mixed with herbs or garlic for extra flavor – and smooth back the skin. To bard poultry, cover the breast with slices of bacon before roasting.

Five Stuffings for Chicken

BASIC HERB STUFFING

INGREDIENTS

1 small onion, finely chopped
1 tablespoon butter
2 cups fresh breadcrumbs
1 tablespoon chopped fresh parsley
1 teaspoon mixed dried herbs
1 egg, beaten
salt and black pepper

Cook the onion gently in the butter until tender. Allow to cool.

Add to the remaining ingredients and then mix thoroughly. Season well with salt and pepper.

VARIATIONS

Any of these ingredients may be added to the basic recipe to vary the flavor of the stuffing, depending on what you have in your fridge and cupboards at home.

1 celery stalk, finely chopped
1 small eating apple, diced
1/2 cup chopped walnuts or almonds
1 tablespoon raisins
1/4 cup chopped dried prunes or apricots
2/3 cup mushrooms, finely chopped
grated rind of 1/2 orange or lemon
1/2 cup pine nuts
2 strips bacon, chopped

APRICOT AND ORANGE STUFFING

INGREDIENTS

1 tablespoon butter
1 small onion, finely chopped
2 cups fresh breadcrumbs
1/4 cup finely chopped dried apricots
grated rind of 1/2 orange
1 small egg, beaten
1 tablespoon chopped fresh parsley
salt and black pepper

Heat the butter in a frying pan and cook the onion gently until tender.

Allow to cool slightly, and add to the rest of the ingredients. Mix until thoroughly combined and season with salt and pepper.

RAISIN AND NUT STUFFING

INGREDIENTS

2 cups fresh breadcrumbs
1/3 cup raisins
1/2 cup walnuts, almonds, pistachios or pine nuts
1 tablespoon chopped fresh parsley
1 teaspoon chopped mixed herbs
1 small egg, beaten
2 tablespoons melted butter
salt and black pepper

Mix all the ingredients together thoroughly. Season well with salt and pepper.

Raisin and Nut Stuffing

PARSLEY, LEMON AND THYME STUFFING

INGREDIENTS

2 cups fresh breadcrumbs
2 tablespoons butter
1 tablespoon chopped fresh parsley
1/2 teaspoon dried thyme
grated rind of 1/4 lemon
1 strip lean bacon, chopped
1 small egg, beaten
salt and black pepper

Mix all the ingredients together to combine them thoroughly.

Parsley, Lemon and Thyme Stuffing

SAUSAGE STUFFING

INGREDIENTS

1 tablespoon butter
1 small onion, finely chopped
2 strips lean bacon, chopped
8 ounces sausage meat
1/2 teaspoon mixed dried herbs
salt and black pepper

Heat the butter in a frying pan and cook the onion until tender. Add the bacon and cook for 5 minutes, then allow to cool.

Add to the remaining ingredients and mix thoroughly.

Making Poultry Stock

A good homemade poultry stock is invaluable in the kitchen. It is simple and economical to make, and can be stored in the freezer for up to 6 months. If poultry giblets are available, add them (except the livers) with the wings.

INGREDIENTS

Makes about 10 cups

$2^{1}/_{2}$–3 pounds poultry wings, backs and necks (chicken, turkey, etc)
2 onions, unpeeled, quartered
7 pints cold water
2 carrots, coarsely chopped
2 celery stalks, with leaves if possible, coarsely chopped
a small handful of fresh parsley
a few fresh thyme sprigs or
$^{3}/_{4}$ teaspoon dried thyme
1 or 2 bay leaves
10 black peppercorns, lightly crushed

1 Combine the poultry wings, backs and necks and the onions in a stockpot. Cook over moderate heat until the poultry and onion pieces are lightly browned, stirring from time to time so they color evenly.

2 Add the water and stir well to mix in the sediment on the bottom of the pot. Bring to a boil and skim off the impurities as they rise to the surface of the stock.

3 Add the remaining ingredients. Partially cover the stockpot and gently simmer the stock for about 3 hours.

4 Strain the stock into a bowl and allow to cool, then refrigerate.

5 When cold, carefully remove the layer of fat that will have settled on the surface.

FRUGAL STOCK

Stock can be made from the bones and carcasses of roasted poultry, cooked with vegetables and flavorings. Save the carcasses in a plastic bag in the freezer until you have three or four, then make stock. It may not have quite as rich a flavor as stock made from a whole bird or fresh wings, backs and necks, but it will still taste fresher and less salty than stock made from a commercial cube.

STOCK TIPS

If desired, use a whole bird for making stock instead of wings, backs and necks. A boiling fowl, if available, will give wonderful flavor and provide meat to use in salads, sandwiches, soups and casseroles.

No salt is added to stock because as the stock reduces, the flavor becomes concentrated and the saltiness increases. Add salt to dishes which contain the stock.

Soups & Appetizers

Smoked Chicken and Lentil Soup

Smoked chicken gives added depth of flavor to this hearty soup.

INGREDIENTS

Serves 4

2 tablespoons butter
1 large carrot, chopped
1 onion, chopped
1 celery stalk, chopped
1 leek, white part only, chopped
$1^1/2$ cups mushrooms, chopped
$^1/4$ cup dry white wine
4 cups homemade or canned chicken stock
2 teaspoons dried thyme
1 bay leaf
$^1/2$ cup lentils
$1^1/2$ cups smoked chicken meat, diced
salt and pepper
chopped fresh parsley, to garnish

1 Melt the butter in a large saucepan. Add the carrot, onion, celery, leek and mushrooms. Cook gently until golden, about 3–5 minutes.

2 Stir in the wine and chicken stock. Bring to a boil and skim any foam that rises to the surface. Add the thyme and bay leaf. Lower the heat, cover, and simmer gently for 30 minutes.

3 Add the lentils and continue cooking, covered, until they are just tender, 30–40 minutes more. Stir the soup occasionally.

4 Stir in the chicken and season to taste. Cook until just heated through. Ladle into bowls and garnish with chopped parsley.

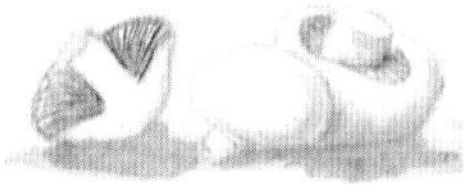

Mulligatawny Soup

Mulligatawny (which means "pepper water") was introduced into England in the late eighteenth century, by members of the army and colonial service returning home from India.

INGREDIENTS

Serves 4

4 tablespoons butter or 4 tablespoons olive oil
2 large chicken joints, about 12 ounces each
1 onion, chopped
1 carrot, chopped
1 small turnip, chopped
about 1 tablespoon curry powder, to taste
4 cloves
6 black peppercorns, lightly crushed
1/4 cup lentils
3 3/4 cups homemade or canned chicken stock
1/4 cup golden raisins
salt and pepper

1 Melt the butter or heat the oil in a large saucepan and brown the chicken over brisk heat. Transfer the chicken onto a plate.

COOK'S TIP

Red split lentils will give the best color for this dish, although green or brown lentils could be used, if you prefer.

2 Add the onion, carrot and turnip to the pan and cook, stirring occasionally, until lightly colored. Stir in the curry powder, cloves and peppercorns and cook for 1–2 minutes. Add the lentils.

3 Pour in the stock and bring to a boil. Add the golden raisins and chicken and any juices from the plate. Cover and simmer gently for about 1 1/4 hours.

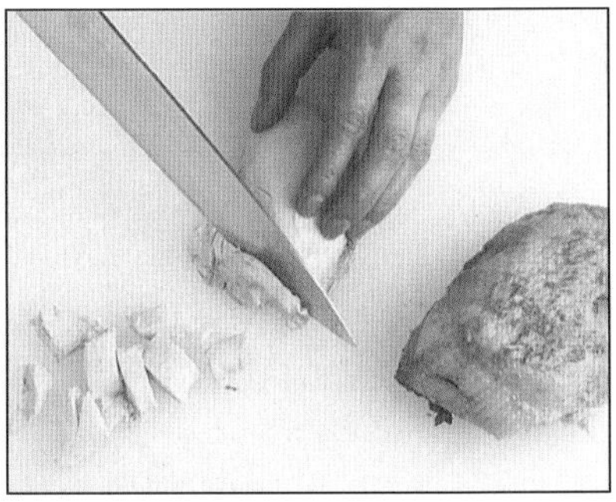

4 Remove the chicken from the pan and discard the skin and bones. Chop the flesh, return to the soup and reheat. Check and adjust the seasoning before serving the soup piping hot.

Chicken Vermicelli Soup with Egg Shreds

This light soup can be put together in a matter of minutes and is full of flavor.

INGREDIENTS

Serves 4–6

3 jumbo eggs
2 tablespoons chopped cilantro or parsley
$6^{1}/_{4}$ cups homemade or canned chicken stock
1 cup dried vermicelli or angel hair pasta
4 ounces cooked chicken breast, sliced
salt and pepper

1 First make the egg shreds. Whisk the eggs together in a small bowl and stir in the chopped cilantro or parsley.

2 Heat a small nonstick frying pan and pour in 2–3 tablespoons beaten egg, swirling to cover the bottom evenly. Cook until set. Repeat until all the mixture is used up.

3 Roll each pancake up and slice thinly into shreds. Set aside.

4 Bring the stock to a boil and add the pasta, breaking it into short lengths. Cook for 3–5 minutes, until the pasta is almost tender, then add the chicken, salt and pepper. Heat through for 2–3 minutes, then stir in the egg shreds. Serve immediately.

Thai Chicken Soup

This filling and tasty soup is very quick to prepare and cook.

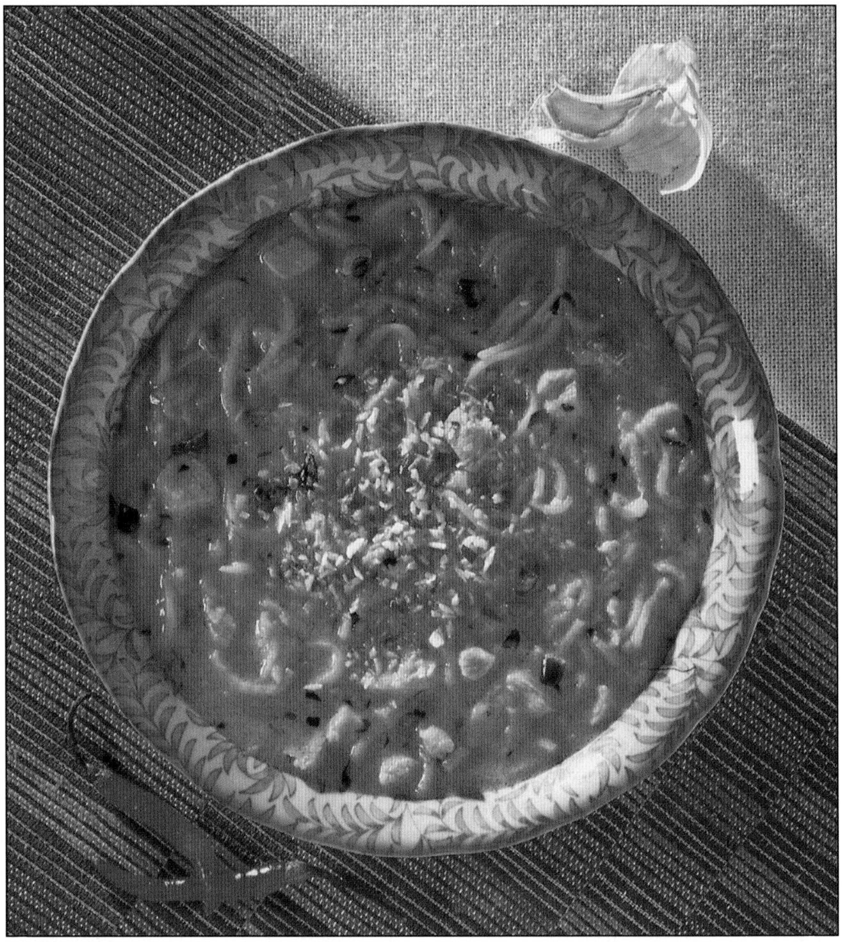

INGREDIENTS

Serves 4

1 tablespoon vegetable oil
1 garlic clove, finely chopped
2 boned chicken breasts, about 6 ounces each, skinned and chopped
$^1/_2$ teaspoon ground turmeric
$^1/_4$ teaspoon hot chili powder
3 ounces creamed coconut
$3^3/_4$ cups hot homemade or canned chicken stock,
2 tablespoons lemon or lime juice
2 tablespoons crunchy peanut butter
1 cup thread egg noodles, broken into small pieces
1 tablespoon scallions, finely chopped
1 tablespoon chopped fresh cilantro
salt and black pepper
2 tablespoons dried coconut and $^1/_2$ fresh red chili, seeded and finely chopped, to garnish

1 Heat the oil in a large pan and si fry the garlic for 1 minute, until lightly golden. Add the chicken and spices and stir-fry for another 3–4 minutes.

2 Crumble the creamed coconut into the hot chicken stock and stir until dissolved. Pour onto the chicken and add the lemon or lime juice, peanut butter and egg noodles.

3 Cover the pan and simmer for about 15 minutes.

4 Add the chopped scallions and cilantro, then season well and cook for another 5 minutes. Meanwhile, place the dried coconut and chili in a small frying pan and heat for 2–3 minutes, stirring frequently.

5 Serve the soup in bowls and sprinkle each one with some fried coconut and hot chili.

Chicken Cigars

These small crispy rolls can be served warm as canapés with a drink before a meal, or as a first course with a crisp, colorful salad.

INGREDIENTS

Serves 4

10-ounce package of filo pastry, defrosted
3 tablespoons olive oil
fresh parsley, to garnish

For the filling

3 cups ground raw chicken
salt and freshly ground black pepper
1 egg, beaten
1/2 teaspoon ground cinnamon
1/2 teaspoon ground ginger
2 tablespoons raisins
1 tablespoon olive oil
1 small onion, finely chopped

1 Mix all the filling ingredients, except the oil and onion, in a bowl. Heat the oil in a large frying pan and cook the onion until tender. Let cool. Add the mixed filling ingredients.

2 Preheat the oven to 350°F. Once the filo pastry package has been opened, keep the pastry covered at all times with a damp dish towel. Work fast, as the filo pastry dries out very quickly when exposed to the air. Unroll the pastry and cut it into 10 x 4 inch strips.

3 Take a strip (cover the remainder), brush with a little oil and place a small spoonful of filling about 1/2 inch from the end.

4 To encase the filling, fold the sides inward to a width of 2 inches and roll into a cigar shape. Place on a greased baking sheet and brush with oil. Repeat to use all the filling. Bake for about 20–25 minutes, until golden brown and crisp. Garnish with fresh parsley and serve.

Chicken Liver Pâté

A deliciously smooth pâté which is ideal to spread on hot toast.

INGREDIENTS

Serves 6 or more

4 tablespoons butter
1 onion, finely chopped
12 ounces chicken livers, trimmed of all dark or greenish parts
4 tablespoons medium sherry
1 ounce cream cheese
1–2 tablespoons lemon juice
2 hard-boiled eggs, chopped
salt and pepper
1/4 cup clarified butter

1 Melt the butter in a frying pan. Add the onion and livers and cook until the onion is soft and the livers are lightly browned and no longer pink in the center.

2 Add the sherry and boil until reduced by half. Cool slightly.

COOK'S TIP

Add brandy instead of sherry for a special occasion dinner party.

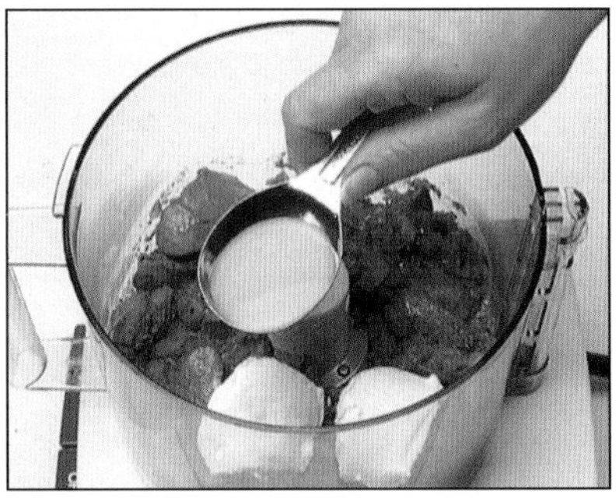

3 Turn the mixture into a food processor or blender and add the cream cheese and 1 tablespoon lemon juice. Blend until smooth.

4 Add the hard-boiled eggs and blend briefly. Season with salt and pepper. Taste and add more lemon juice, if desired.

5 Pack the liver pâté into a mold or into individual ramekins. Smooth the surface.

6 Spoon a layer of clarified butter over the surface of the pâté. Chill until firm. Serve at room temperature, with hot toast or crackers.

Chicken and Avocado Mayonnaise

You need really firm scoops or forks to eat this appetizer, so don't be tempted to try to pass it around as a finger food.

INGREDIENTS

Serves 4

2 tablespoons mayonnaise
1 tablespoon ricotta or farmer's cheese
2 garlic cloves, crushed
1 cup chopped cooked chicken
1 large ripe, but firm, avocado, peeled and pitted
2 tablespoons lemon juice
salt and black pepper
corn chips or tortilla chips, to serve

1 Mix together the mayonnaise, ricotta, garlic, and seasoning to taste, in a small bowl. Stir in the chopped chicken.

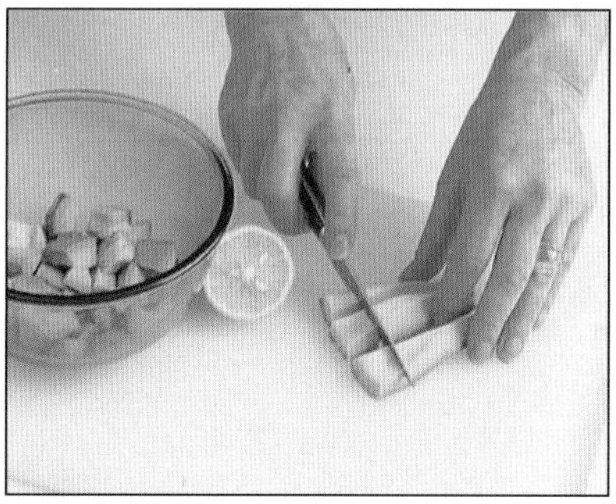

2 Chop the avocado and toss immediately in lemon juice.

3 Mix the avocado gently into the chicken mixture. Check the seasoning and chill until needed.

4 Serve in small serving dishes with the corn or tortilla chips as scoops, if desired.

COOK'S TIP

This mixture also makes a great, chunky filling for sandwiches, rolls or pita bread. Or, serve as a main course salad, heaped onto a base of mixed salad leaves.

Meals in Minutes

Monday Savory Omelet

Use up all your leftover odds and ends in this tasty omelet.

INGREDIENTS

Serves 4–6

2 tablespoons olive oil
1 large onion, chopped
2 large garlic cloves, crushed
4 ounces rindless bacon, chopped
2 ounces cold cooked chicken, chopped
4 ounces leftover cooked vegetables (preferably ones which are not too soft)
1 cup leftover cooked rice or pasta
4 eggs
2 tablespoons chopped, mixed fresh herbs, such as parsley, chives, marjoram or tarragon, or 2 teaspoons dried
1 teaspoon Worcestershire sauce, or more to taste
1 tablespoon grated aged Cheddar cheese
salt and black pepper

1 Heat the oil in a large flameproof frying pan and sauté the onion, garlic and bacon until all the fat has run out of the bacon.

2 Add the chopped chicken, vegetables and rice (or pasta). Beat the eggs, herbs and Worcestershire sauce together with seasoning. Pour over the rice (or pasta) and vegetables, stir lightly, then leave the mixture undisturbed to cook gently for about 5 minutes.

3 When just beginning to set, sprinkle with the cheese and place under a preheated broiler until just firm and golden.

COOK'S TIP

This is surprisingly good cold, so it's perfect for taking on picnics, or using for packed lunches.

Tagliatelle with Chicken and Herb Sauce

This wine-flavored sauce is best served with green salad.

INGREDIENTS

Serves 4

2 tablespoons olive oil
1 red onion, cut into wedges
12 ounces tagliatelle
1 garlic clove, chopped
$2^{1}/_{2}$ cups chicken, diced
$1^{1}/_{4}$ cups dry vermouth
3 tablespoons chopped fresh mixed herbs
$^{2}/_{3}$ cup ricotta or farmer's cheese
salt and black pepper
shredded fresh mint, to garnish

1 Heat the oil in a large frying pan and fry the onion for 10 minutes until softened, and the layers begin to separate.

2 Cook the pasta in plenty of water, following the instructions on the package.

3 Add the garlic and chicken to the frying pan and fry for 10 minutes, stirring occasionally, until the chicken is browned all over and cooked through.

4 Pour in the vermouth, bring to a boil and boil rapidly until reduced by about half.

5 Stir in the herbs, cheese and seasoning and heat through gently, but do not boil.

6 Drain the pasta thoroughly and toss it with the sauce to coat. Serve immediately, garnished with shredded fresh mint.

COOK'S TIP

If you don't want to use vermouth, use dry white wine instead. Orvieto and frascati are two Italian wines that are ideal to use in this sauce.

Penne with Chicken and Ham Sauce

A meal in itself, this colorful pasta sauce is perfect for lunch or dinner.

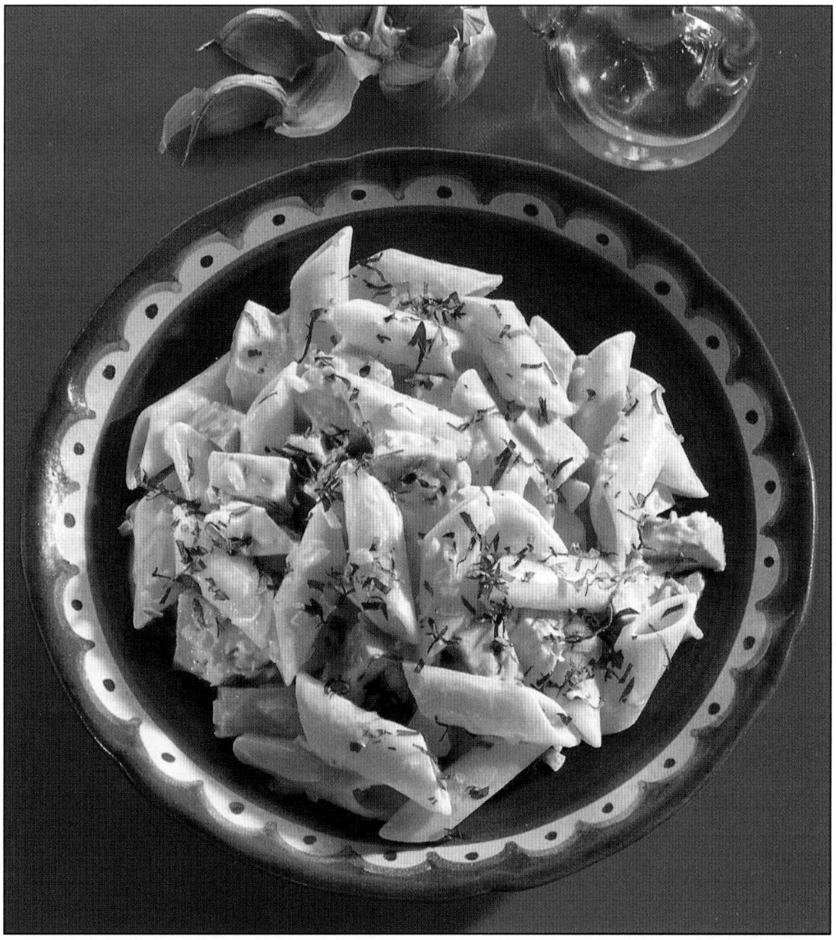

INGREDIENTS

Serves 4

3 cups penne
2 tablespoons butter
1 onion, chopped
1 garlic clove, chopped
1 bay leaf
2 cups dry white wine
$^2/_3$ cup crème fraîche
$1^1/_2$ cups cooked chicken, skinned, boned and diced
$^2/_3$ cup cooked lean ham, diced
1 cup grated Gouda cheese
1 tablespoon chopped fresh mint
salt and black pepper
finely shredded fresh mint, to garnish

1 Cook the pasta in plenty of water, following the instructions on the package.

2 Heat the butter in a large frying pan and fry the onion for 10 minutes, until softened.

3 Add the garlic, bay leaf and wine and bring to a boil. Boil rapidly until reduced by half. Remove the bay leaf, then stir in the crème fraîche and bring back to a boil.

4 Add the chicken, ham and cheese and simmer for 5 minutes, stirring occasionally, until heated through.

5 Add the mint and seasoning. Drain the pasta and turn it into a large serving bowl. Toss with the sauce immediately and garnish with shredded mint.

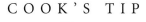

COOK'S TIP

Crème fraîche is a richer, full-fat French cream with a slightly acidic taste. If you can't find any, substitute sour cream.

Chicken and Shiitake Mushroom Pizza

The addition of shiitake mushrooms adds an earthy flavor to this colorful pizza, while fresh red chili gives a hint of spiciness.

INGREDIENTS

Serves 3–4

3 tablespoons olive oil
3 cups chicken breast fillets, skinned and cut into thin strips
1 bunch scallions, sliced
1 fresh red chili, seeded and chopped
1 red bell pepper, seeded and cut into thin strips
3 ounces fresh shiitake mushrooms, wiped and sliced
3–4 tablespoons chopped fresh cilantro
1 pizza crust, about 10–12 inches diameter
1 tablespoon chili oil
1 1/4 cups mozzarella cheese
salt and black pepper

1 Preheat the oven to 425°F. Heat 2 tablespoons of the olive oil in a wok or large frying pan. Add the chicken, scallions, chili, pepper and mushrooms and stir-fry over high heat for 2–3 minutes, until the chicken is firm but still slightly pink in the center. Season with salt and pepper.

2 Pour off any excess oil, then set aside the chicken mixture until cool.

3 Stir the fresh cilantro into the chicken mixture.

4 Brush the pizza crust with the chili oil.

5 Spoon on the chicken mixture and drizzle on the remaining olive oil.

6 Grate the mozzarella and sprinkle on. Bake for 15–20 minutes, until crisp and golden. Serve immediately.

Chicken and Avocado Pita Pizzas

Pita bread is used here to make quick crusts for a tasty pizza.

INGREDIENTS

Serves 4

8 plum tomatoes, quartered
3–4 tablespoons olive oil
1 large ripe avocado
8 pita bread rounds
6–7 slices of cooked chicken, chopped
1 onion, thinly sliced
$2^1/_2$ cups grated Cheddar cheese
2 tablespoons chopped fresh cilantro
salt and pepper

1 Preheat the oven to 450°F.

2 Place the quartered tomatoes in a baking dish. Drizzle with 1 tablespoon of the oil and season to taste. Bake for 30 minutes; do not stir.

3 Remove the baking dish from the oven and mash the tomatoes with a fork, removing the skins as you mash. Set aside.

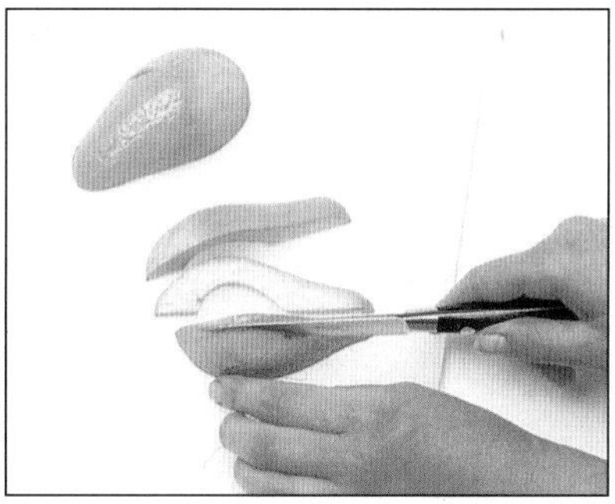

4 Peel and pit the avocado. Cut into 16 thin slices.

5 Brush the edges of the pita breads with oil. Arrange the breads on two baking sheets.

6 Spread each pita with mashed tomato, almost to the edges.

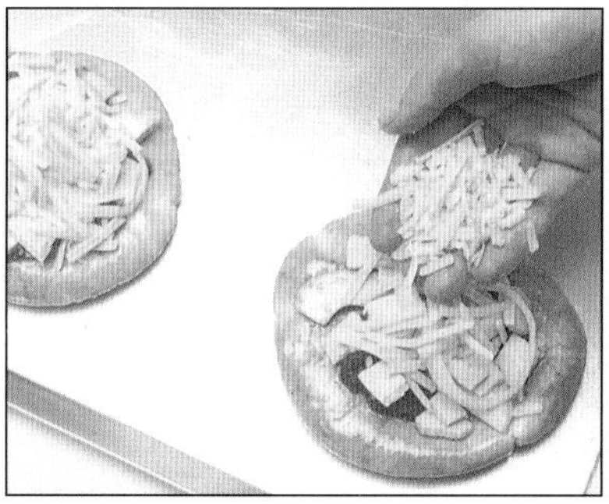

7 Top each with 2 avocado slices. Sprinkle with the chicken, then add a few onion slices. Season to taste. Sprinkle on the cheese.

8 Place one sheet in the middle of the oven and bake until the cheese begins to melt, about 15–20 minutes. Sprinkle with half the cilantro and serve. Meanwhile, bake the second batch of pizzas, and serve them hot.

Chicken with Bell Peppers

This colorful dish comes from the south of Italy, where sweet peppers are plentiful.

INGREDIENTS

Serves 4

1 chicken, 3 pounds, cut into serving pieces
3 large bell peppers, red, yellow or green
6 tablespoons olive oil
2 medium red onions, finely sliced
2 cloves garlic, finely chopped
small piece of dried chili, crumbled (optional)
1/2 cup white wine
salt and black pepper
2 tomatoes, fresh or canned, peeled and chopped
3 tablespoons chopped fresh parsley

1 Trim any fat off the chicken, and remove all excess skin. Prepare peppers by cutting them in half and discarding the seeds and the stem. Slice into strips.

2 Heat half the oil in a large heavy saucepan or casserole. Add the onions, and cook over low heat until soft. Remove to a side dish. Add the remaining oil to the pan, raise the heat to medium, add the chicken and brown on all sides, 6–8 minutes. Return the onions to the pan, and add the garlic and dried chili, if using.

3 Pour in the wine, and cook until it has reduced by half. Add the peppers and stir well to coat them with the oil. Season. After 3–4 minutes, stir in the tomatoes. Lower the heat, cover the pan, and cook until the peppers are soft, and the chicken is cooked, about 25–30 minutes. Stir occasionally. Stir in the chopped parsley and serve.

Chicken Breasts Cooked in Butter

This simple and very delicious way of cooking chicken brings out all of its delicacy.

INGREDIENTS

Serves 4

4 small chicken breasts, skinned and boned
flour seasoned with salt and freshly ground black pepper, for dredging
6 tablespoons butter
1 sprig fresh parsley, to garnish

1 Separate the two fillets of each breast. They come apart very easily; one is large, the other small. Pound the large fillets between two sheets of plastic wrap lightly to flatten them. Dredge the chicken in the seasoned flour, shaking off any excess.

2 Heat the butter in a large heavy frying pan until it bubbles. Place all the chicken fillets in the pan, in one layer if possible. Cook over medium to high heat for 3–4 minutes, until they are golden brown.

3 Turn the chicken over. Reduce the heat to low to medium, and continue cooking until the fillets are cooked through but still springy to the touch, about 9–12 minutes in all. If the chicken begins to brown too much, cover the pan for the final minutes of cooking. Serve immediately garnished with a little parsley.

Pan-fried Honey Chicken Drumsticks

The sweetness of the honey contrasts well with the lemon and soy sauce.

INGREDIENTS

Serves 4

- 1/2 cup honey
- juice of 1 lemon
- 2 tablespoons soy sauce
- 1 tablespoon sesame seeds
- 1/2 teaspoon fresh or dried thyme leaves
- 12 chicken drumsticks
- 1/2 teaspoon salt
- 1/2 teaspoon pepper
- 3/4 cup all-purpose flour
- 3 tablespoons butter or margarine
- 3 tablespoons vegetable oil
- 1/2 cup white wine
- 1/2 cup homemade or canned chicken stock

1 In a large bowl, combine the honey, lemon juice, soy sauce, sesame seeds and thyme. Add the chicken drumsticks and mix to coat them well. Let marinate in a cool place for 2 hours or more, turning occasionally.

2 Mix the salt, pepper and flour in a shallow bowl. Drain the drumsticks, reserving the marinade. Roll them in the seasoned flour to coat all over.

3 Heat the butter or margarine with the oil in a large frying pan. When hot and sizzling, add the drumsticks. Brown them on all sides. Reduce the heat to medium–low and cook until the chicken is done, 12–15 minutes.

4 Test the drumsticks with a fork; the juices should run clear. Remove the drumsticks to a serving platter and keep hot.

5 Pour off most of the fat from the pan. Add the wine, stock and reserved marinade and stir well to mix in the cooking juices on the bottom of the pan. Bring to a boil and simmer until reduced by half. Check and adjust the seasoning, then spoon the sauce over the drumsticks and serve.

Louisiana Rice

A tasty meal of pork, rice, chicken livers and an array of spices.

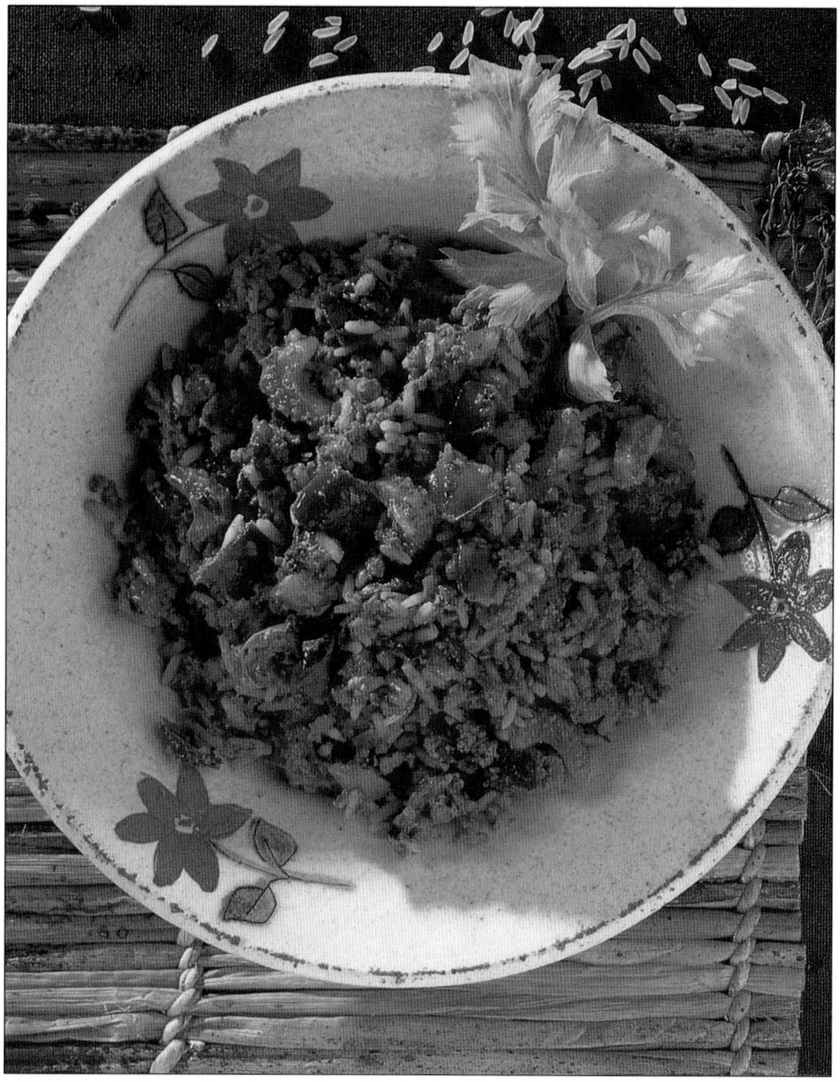

INGREDIENTS

Serves 4

4 tablespoons vegetable oil
1 small eggplant, diced
8 ounces ground pork
1 green bell pepper, seeded and chopped
2 stalks celery, chopped
1 onion, chopped
1 garlic clove, crushed
1 teaspoon cayenne pepper
1 teaspoon paprika
1 teaspoon black pepper
1/2 teaspoon salt
1 teaspoon dried thyme
1/2 teaspoon dried oregano
2 cups homemade or canned chicken stock
8 ounces chicken livers, minced
3/4 cup long-grain rice
1 bay leaf
3 tablespoons chopped fresh parsley
celery leaves, to garnish

1 Heat the oil in a frying pan until really hot, then add the diced eggplant and stir-fry for about 5 minutes.

2 Add the pork and cook for about 6–8 minutes, until browned, using a wooden spoon to break any lumps.

3 Add the chopped green pepper, celery, onion, garlic and all the spices and herbs. Cover and cook over high heat for 5–6 minutes, stirring frequently from the bottom to scrape up and distribute the crispy brown bits.

4 Pour on the chicken stock and stir to clean the bottom of the pan. Cover and cook for 6 minutes over medium heat. Stir in the chicken livers, cook for 2 minutes, then stir in the rice and add the bay leaf.

5 Reduce the heat, cover and simmer for about 6–7 minutes. Turn off the heat and let stand for another 10–15 minutes, until the rice is tender. Remove the bay leaf and stir in the chopped parsley. Serve the rice hot, garnished with the celery leaves.

Stir-fried Chicken with Snow Peas

Juicy chicken stir-fried with snow peas, cashews and water chestnuts.

INGREDIENTS

Serves 4

2 tablespoons sesame oil
6 tablespoons lemon juice
1 garlic clove, crushed
1/2-inch piece fresh ginger, peeled and grated
1 teaspoon honey
1 pound chicken breast fillets, cut into strips
4 ounces snow peas, trimmed
2 tablespoons peanut oil
1/2 cup cashews
6 scallions, cut into strips
1 can (8-ounces) water chestnuts, drained and thinly sliced
salt
saffron rice, to serve

1 Mix together the sesame oil, lemon juice, garlic, ginger and honey in a shallow non-metallic dish. Add the chicken and mix well. Cover and let marinate for at least 3–4 hours.

2 Blanch the snow peas in boiling salted water for 1 minute. Drain and refresh under cold running water.

3 Drain the chicken strips and reserve the marinade. Heat the peanut oil in a wok or large frying pan, add the cashews and stir-fry for about 1–2 minutes until golden brown. Remove the cashews from the wok or frying pan, using a slotted spoon, and set aside.

4 Add the chicken and stir-fry for 3–4 minutes, until golden brown. Add the scallions, snow peas, water chestnuts and the reserved marinade. Cook for a few minutes, until the chicken is tender and the sauce is bubbling and hot. Stir in the cashews and serve with saffron rice.

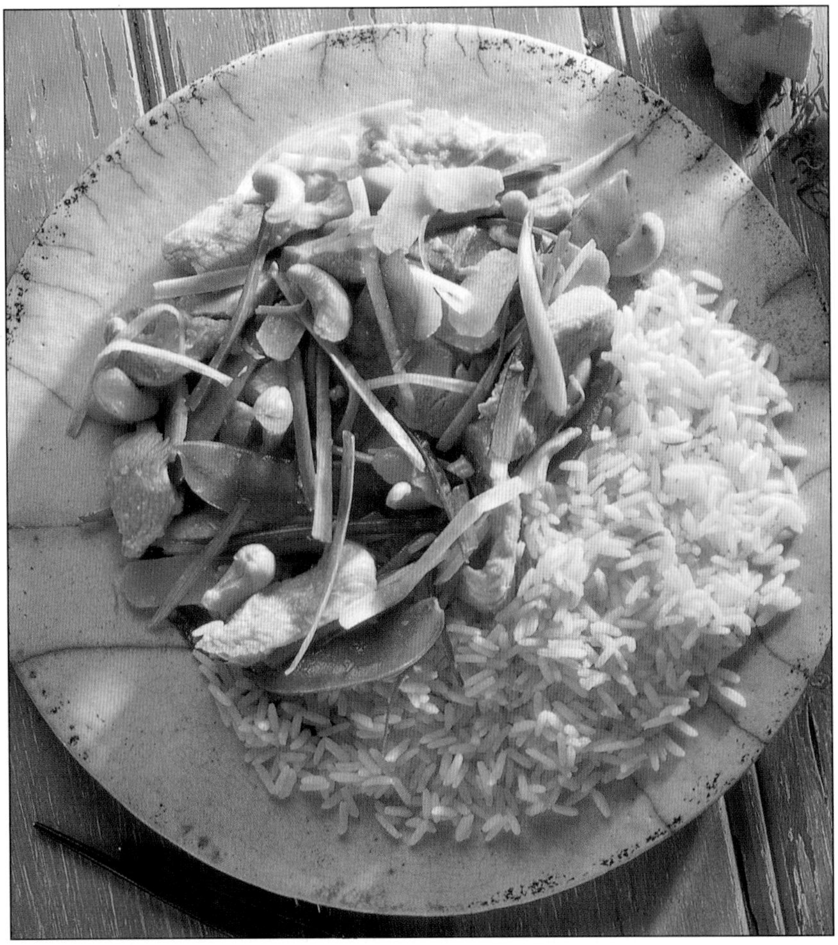

Risotto

An Italian dish made with short grain arborio rice, which gives a creamy consistency to this easy one-pan recipe.

INGREDIENTS

Serves 4

1 tablespoon oil
1 cup arborio rice
1 onion, chopped
2 cups ground chicken
2 1/2 cups homemade or canned chicken stock
1 red bell pepper, seeded and chopped
1 yellow bell pepper, seeded and chopped
3/4 cup frozen green beans
1 1/2 cups Crimini mushrooms, sliced
1 tablespoon chopped fresh parsley
salt and black pepper
fresh parsley, to garnish

1 Heat the oil in a large frying pan. Add the rice and cook for 2 minutes, until transparent.

2 Add the onion and ground chicken. Cook for 5 minutes, stirring occasionally.

3 Pour in the stock and bring to a boil.

4 Stir in the peppers and reduce the heat. Cook for 10 minutes.

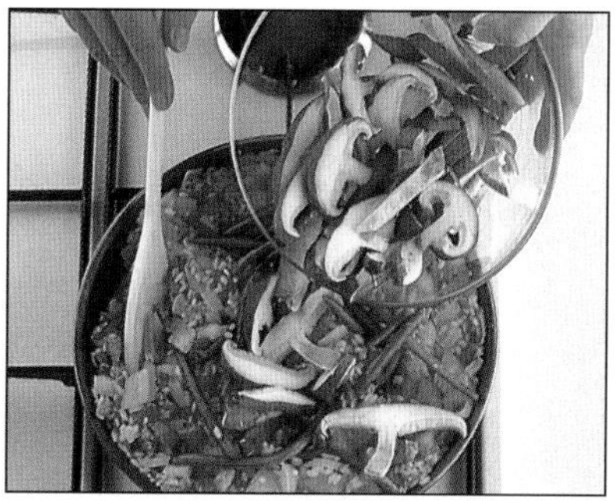

5 Add the green beans and mushrooms and cook for another 10 minutes.

6 Stir in the fresh parsley and season well to taste. Cook for 10 minutes, or until the liquid has been absorbed. Serve garnished with fresh parsley.

Chicken in Green Sauce

Slow, gentle cooking makes the chicken succulent and tender.

INGREDIENTS

Serves 4

2 tablespoons butter
1 tablespoon olive oil
4 chicken portions
1 small onion, finely chopped
$^2/_3$ cup medium dry white wine
$^2/_3$ cup homemade or canned chicken stock
6 ounces watercress
2 thyme sprigs and 2 tarragon sprigs
$^2/_3$ cup heavy cream
salt and black pepper
watercress leaves, to garnish

1 Heat the butter and oil in a heavy shallow pan, then brown the chicken evenly. Transfer the chicken to a plate, using a slotted spoon, and keep warm in the oven.

2 Add the onion to the cooking juices in the pan and cook until softened but not colored.

3 Stir in the wine, boil for 2–3 minutes, then add the stock and bring to a boil. Return the chicken to the pan, cover tightly and cook very gently for about 30 minutes, until the chicken juices run clear. Then transfer the chicken to a warm dish, cover the dish and keep warm.

4 Boil the cooking juices hard until reduced to about 4 tablespoons. Add the leaves from the watercress and herbs to the pan with the cream and simmer over medium heat until the sauce has thickened slightly.

5 Return the cooked chicken to the casserole, season and heat through for a few minutes. Garnish with watercress leaves before serving.

Chicken Stroganoff

Based on the classic Russian dish, usually made with beef. Serve with rice mixed with chopped celery and scallions.

INGREDIENTS

Serves 4

4 large chicken breasts, boned and skinned
3 tablespoons olive oil
1 large onion, thinly sliced
3 cups mushrooms, sliced
1¼ cups sour cream
salt and black pepper
1 tablespoon chopped fresh parsley, to garnish

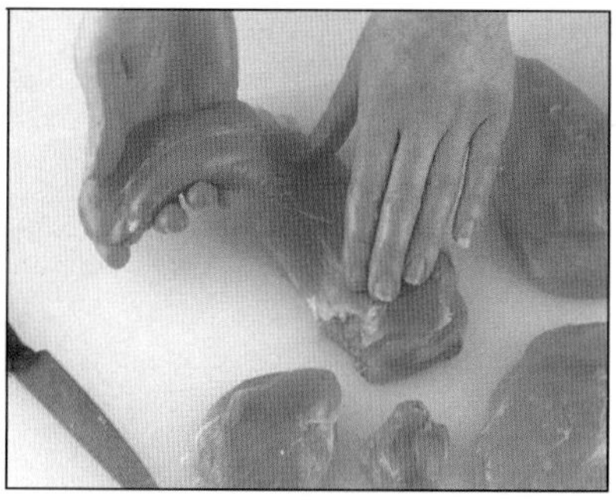

1 Split the chicken breasts into two natural fillets, place between two sheets of plastic wrap and flatten each to a thickness of ½ inch with a rolling pin.

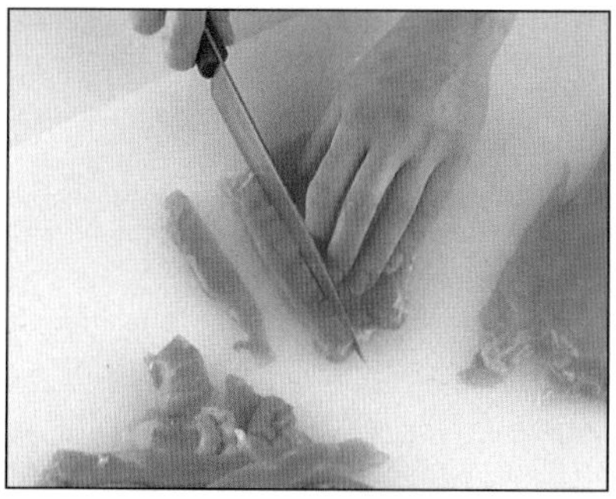

2 Cut into 1-inch strips diagonally across the fillets.

3 Heat 2 tablespoons of the oil in a frying pan and cook the onion slowly until soft but not colored.

4 Add the mushrooms and cook until golden brown. Remove and keep warm.

5 Increase the heat, add the remaining oil and fry the chicken very quickly, in small batches, for 3–4 minutes, until lightly colored. Remove to a dish and keep warm.

6 Return all the chicken, onions and mushrooms to the pan and season with salt and black pepper. Stir in the sour cream and bring to a boil. Sprinkle with fresh parsley and serve immediately.

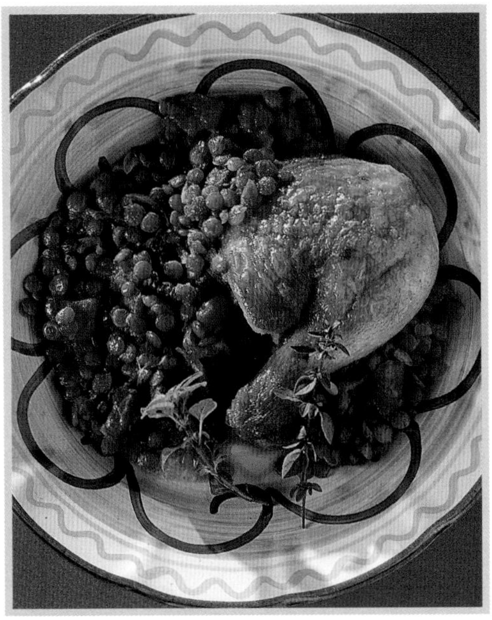

Casseroles & Bakes

Cannelloni al Forno

A lighter alternative to the usual beef-filled, béchamel-coated version. Fill with ricotta, onions and mushrooms for a vegetarian recipe.

INGREDIENTS

Serves 4–6

4 cups skinned and boned chicken breast, cooked
2 $^{1}/_{2}$ cups mushrooms
2 garlic cloves, crushed
2 tablespoons chopped fresh parsley
1 tablespoon chopped fresh tarragon
1 egg, beaten
fresh lemon juice
12–18 cannelloni tubes
2 cups homemade or canned tomato sauce
$^{2}/_{3}$ cup freshly grated Parmesan cheese
salt and pepper
1 sprig fresh parsley, to garnish

1 Preheat the oven to 400°F. Place the chicken in a blender or food processor and blend until finely ground. Transfer to a bowl.

2 Place the mushrooms, garlic, parsley and tarragon in the food processor and blend until finely ground.

3 Beat the mushroom mixture into the chicken mixture thoroughly, then add the egg, salt and pepper and lemon juice to taste and mix well.

4 If necessary, cook the cannelloni in plenty of salted boiling water according to the instructions, then drain well on a clean dish towel.

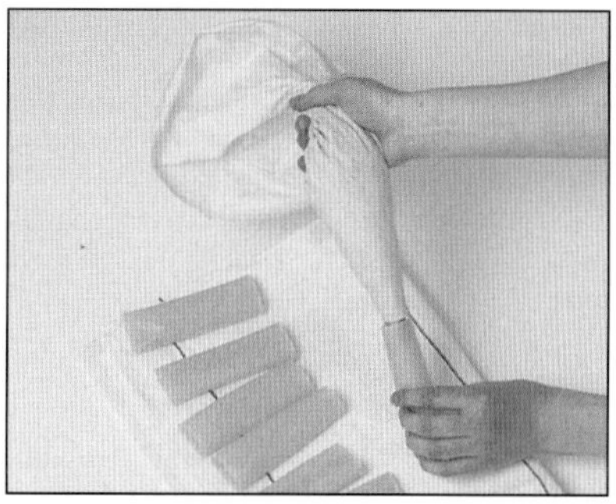

5 Place the filling in a pastry bag fitted with a large plain nozzle. Use this to fill each tube of cannelloni, once they are cool enough to handle.

6 Lay the filled cannelloni tightly together in a single layer in a buttered shallow ovenproof dish. Spoon the tomato sauce over them and sprinkle with Parmesan cheese. Bake in the oven for 30 minutes, or until brown and bubbling. Serve garnished with a sprig of parsley.

Koftas in Tomato Sauce

Delicious meatballs in a rich tomato sauce. Serve with pasta and grated Parmesan cheese, if desired.

INGREDIENTS

Serves 4

$1^1/2$ pounds chicken
1 onion, grated
1 garlic clove, crushed
1 tablespoon chopped fresh parsley
$^1/2$ teaspoon ground cumin
$^1/2$ teaspoon ground coriander
1 egg, beaten
seasoned flour, for rolling
$^1/4$ cup olive oil
salt and black pepper
chopped fresh parsley, to garnish

For the tomato sauce

1 tablespoon butter
2 tablespoons all-purpose flour
1 cup homemade or canned chicken stock
14-ounce can chopped tomatoes, with their juice
1 teaspoon sugar
$^1/4$ teaspoon dried mixed herbs

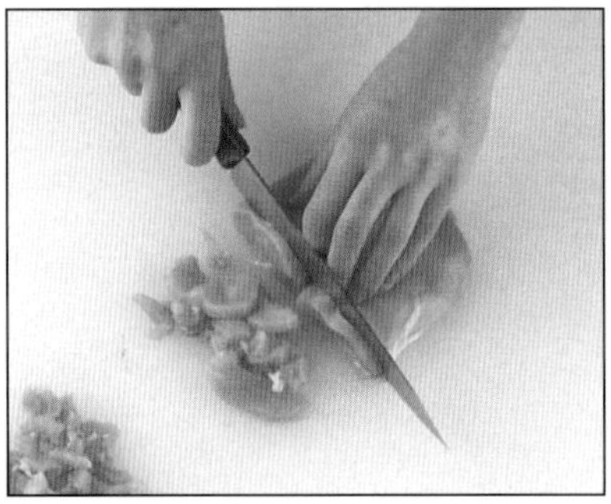

1 Preheat the oven to 350°F. Remove any skin and bone from the chicken and grind or chop finely.

2 Put into a bowl together with the onion, garlic, parsley, spices, seasoning and beaten egg.

3 Mix thoroughly and shape into $1^1/2$-inch balls. Roll lightly in seasoned flour.

4 Heat the oil in a frying pan and brown the balls in small batches (this keeps the oil temperature hot and prevents the flour from becoming soggy). Remove and drain on paper towels. There is no need to cook the balls any longer at this stage, as they will cook in the tomato sauce.

5 To make the tomato sauce, melt the butter in a large saucepan. Add the flour, and then blend in the stock and tomatoes along with their juice. Add the sugar and mixed herbs. Bring to a boil, cover and simmer for 10–15 minutes.

6 Place the browned chicken balls into a shallow ovenproof dish and pour on the tomato sauce, cover with foil and bake in the preheated oven for 30–40 minutes. Adjust the seasoning to taste and sprinkle with parsley.

Tuscan Chicken

This simple peasant casserole has all the flavors of traditional Tuscan food. The wine can be replaced by chicken stock.

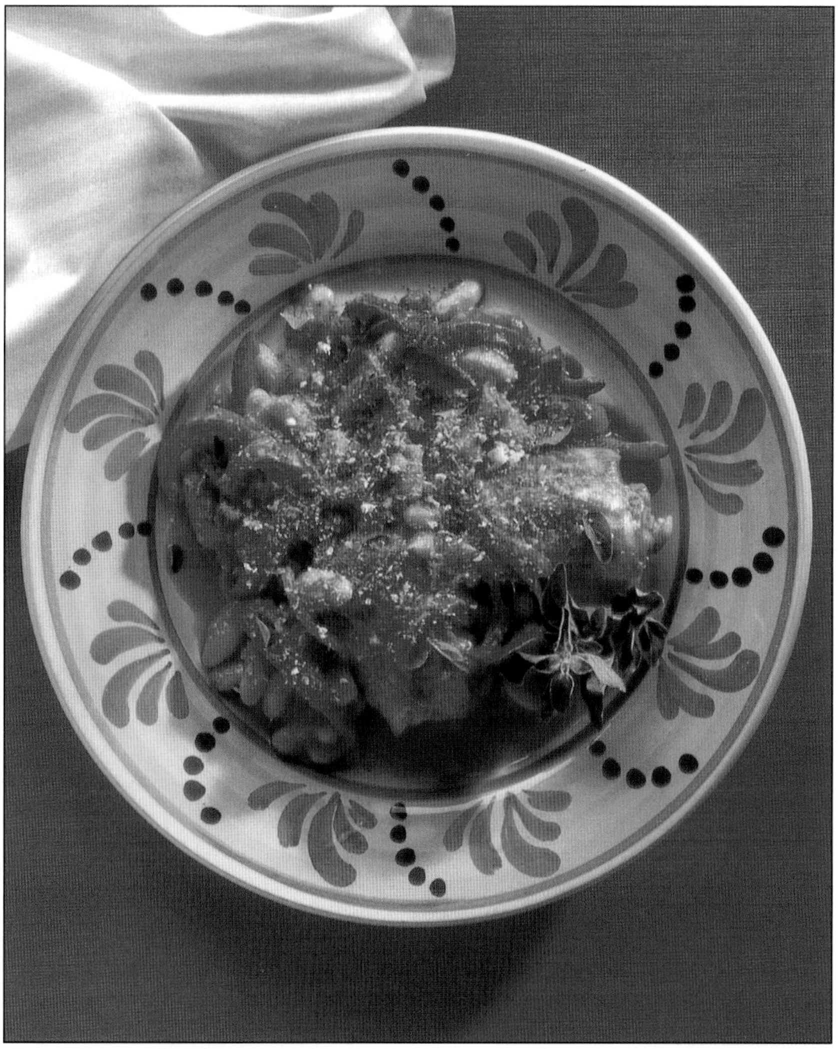

INGREDIENTS

Serves 4

8 chicken thighs, skinned
1 teaspoon olive oil
1 medium onion, thinly sliced
2 red bell peppers, seeded and sliced
1 garlic clove, crushed
$1^{1}/_{4}$ cups puréed tomatoes
$^{2}/_{3}$ cup dry white wine
large sprig fresh oregano, or 1 teaspoon dried oregano
14-ounce can cannellini beans, drained
3 tablespoons fresh breadcrumbs
salt and black pepper

1 Fry the chicken in the oil in a nonstick or heavy pan until golden brown. Remove and keep hot. Add the onion and peppers to the pan and gently sauté until softened, but not brown. Stir in the garlic.

2 Add the chicken, puréed tomatoes, wine and oregano. Season well, bring to a boil, then cover the pan tightly.

3 Lower the heat and simmer gently, stirring occasionally, for 30–35 minutes, or until the chicken is tender and the juices run clear, not pink, when pierced with the point of a knife.

4 Stir in the cannellini beans and simmer for another 5 minutes until heated through. Sprinkle with the breadcrumbs and cook under a hot broiler until golden brown.

Chili Chicken Couscous

Couscous is a convenient alternative to rice and makes a good base for all kinds of ingredients.

INGREDIENTS

Serves 4

2 cups couscous
4 cups boiling water
1 teaspoon olive oil
14 ounces chicken without skin and bone, diced
1 yellow bell pepper, seeded and sliced
2 large zucchini, sliced thickly
1 small green chili, thinly sliced, or 1 teaspoon chili sauce
1 large tomato, diced
15-ounce can chickpeas, drained
salt and black pepper
cilantro or parsley sprigs to garnish

1 Place the couscous in a large bowl and pour boiling water over it. Cover and let stand for 30 minutes.

2 Heat the oil in a large, nonstick pan and stir-fry the chicken quickly, then reduce the heat.

3 Stir in the pepper, zucchini and chili or sauce and cook for about 10 minutes, until the vegetables are softened.

4 Stir in the tomato and chickpeas, then add the couscous. Adjust the seasoning and stir over medium heat until hot. Serve garnished with sprigs of fresh cilantro or parsley.

Chicken Bean Bake

Sliced eggplant layered with beans and chicken and topped with yogurt.

INGREDIENTS

Serves 4

1 medium eggplant, thinly sliced
1 tablespoon olive oil, for brushing
1 pound boneless chicken breast, diced
1 medium onion, chopped
14-ounce can chopped tomatoes
15-ounce can red kidney beans, drained
1 tablespoon paprika
1 tablespoon chopped fresh thyme, or 1 teaspoon dried
1 teaspoon chili sauce
1 1/2 cups strained plain yogurt
1/2 teaspoon nutmeg
salt and black pepper

1 Preheat the oven to 375°F. Arrange the eggplant in a colander and sprinkle with salt.

2 Set the eggplant aside for 30 minutes, then rinse and pat dry. Brush a nonstick pan with oil and fry the eggplant in batches, turning once, until golden.

3 Remove the eggplant, add the chicken and onion to the pan, and cook until lightly browned. Stir in the tomatoes, beans, paprika, thyme, chili sauce and seasoning. In a bowl, combine the yogurt and nutmeg.

4 Layer the meat and eggplant in an ovenproof dish, finishing with eggplant. Spread the yogurt

evenly over the top and bake for 50–60 minutes, until golden.

Chicken Lasagne

Based on the Italian beef lasagne, this is an excellent dish for entertaining guests of all ages. Serve simply with a green salad.

INGREDIENTS

Serves 8

2 tablespoons olive oil
2 pounds ground chicken
1 1/2 cups rindless lean bacon strips, chopped
2 garlic cloves, crushed
1 pound leeks, sliced
1 1/4 cups carrots, diced
2 tablespoons tomato paste
2 cups homemade/canned chicken stock
12 sheets (no need to pre-cook) green lasagne

For the cheese sauce

4 tablespoons butter
1/2 cup all-purpose flour
2 1/2 cups milk
1 cup grated aged Cheddar cheese
1/4 teaspoon dry English mustard
salt and black pepper

1 Heat the oil in a large flame-proof casserole and brown the ground chicken and bacon briskly, separating the pieces with a wooden spoon. Add the crushed garlic cloves, sliced leeks and diced carrots and cook for about 5 minutes until softened. Add the tomato paste, stock and seasoning. Bring to a boil, cover and simmer for 30 minutes.

2 To make the sauce, melt the butter in a saucepan, add the flour and gradually blend in the milk, stirring until smooth. Bring to a boil, stirring all the time, until thickened and simmer for several minutes. Add half the grated cheese and the mustard, and season to taste.

3 Preheat the oven to 375°F. Layer the chicken mixture, lasagne and half the cheese sauce in a 10-cup ovenproof dish, starting and finishing with a layer of chicken.

4 Pour the remaining half of the cheese sauce over the top to cover, sprinkle on the remaining cheese and bake in the preheated oven for 1 hour, or until bubbling and lightly browned on top.

Chicken with Herbs and Lentils

Chicken baked on lentils and served topped with garlic butter.

INGREDIENTS

Serves 4

4-ounce piece of thick bacon, rind removed, chopped
1 large onion, sliced
2 cups well-flavored homemade or canned chicken stock
bay leaf
2 sprigs each parsley, marjoram and thyme
1 cup green or brown lentils
4 chicken portions
salt and black pepper
2–4 tablespoons garlic butter

COOK'S TIP

For economy's sake buy a smallish chicken and cut it in quarters, to give generous portions.

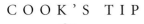

1 Fry the bacon gently in a large, heavy-bottomed flameproof casserole until all the fat runs out and the bacon begins to brown. Add the onion and fry for about another 2 minutes.

2 Stir in the chicken stock, bay leaf, herb stalks and some of the leafy parts (keep some herb sprigs for garnish), lentils and seasoning. Preheat the oven to 375°F.

3 Fry the chicken portions in a frying pan to brown the skin before placing on top of the lentils. Sprinkle with seasoning and some of the herbs.

4 Cover the casserole and cook in the oven for about 40 minutes. Serve with a knob of garlic butter on each portion and a few of the remaining herb sprigs.

Chicken Bobotie

Perfect for a buffet party, this mild curry dish is set with savory custard, which makes serving easy. Serve with boiled rice and chutney.

INGREDIENTS

Serves 8

two thick slices white bread
$1^3/_4$ cups milk
2 tablespoons olive oil
2 medium onions, finely chopped
3 tablespoons medium curry powder
$2^1/_2$ pounds ground chicken
1 tablespoon apricot jam, chutney or sugar
2 tablespoons wine vinegar or lemon juice
3 large eggs, beaten
$^1/_3$ cup dark or golden raisins
12 whole almonds
salt and black pepper

1 Preheat the oven to 350°F. Soak the bread in $^2/_3$ cup of the milk. Heat the oil in a frying pan and gently fry the onions until tender then add the curry powder and cook for another 2 minutes.

2 Add the ground chicken and brown all over, separating the grains of meat as they brown. Remove from the heat and season with salt and black pepper. Add the apricot jam, chutney or sugar and the wine vinegar or lemon juice.

3 Mash the bread in the milk and add to the pan with one of the beaten eggs and the raisins.

4 Grease a 6-cup shallow ovenproof dish with butter. Spoon in the chicken mixture and level the top. Cover with buttered foil and bake in the oven for 30 minutes.

5 Meanwhile, beat the remaining eggs and milk. Remove the dish from the oven and lower the temperature to 300°F. Break up the meat using a fork and pour the egg mixture on top.

6 Scatter on the almonds and bake, uncovered, for 30 minutes until set and brown.

Oat-crusted Chicken with Sage

Oats make a good coating for savory foods, and here they offer a tasty way to add extra fiber.

INGREDIENTS

Serves 4

3 tablespoons skim milk
2 teaspoons English mustard
1/2 cup rolled oats
3 tablespoons chopped sage leaves
8 chicken thighs or drumsticks, skinned
1/2 cup low-fat cream or farmer's cheese
1 teaspoon whole-grain mustard
salt and black pepper
fresh sage leaves, to garnish

COOK'S TIP

If fresh sage is not available, choose another fresh herb, such as thyme or parsley, rather than a dried alternative.

1 Preheat the oven to 400°F. Mix together the milk and English mustard.

2 Mix the oats with 2 tablespoons of the sage and the seasoning on a plate. Brush the chicken with the milk and roll it in the oats.

3 Place the chicken on a baking sheet and bake for about 40 minutes, or until the juices run clear, not pink, when pierced through the thickest part.

4 Meanwhile, combine the low-fat cheese, whole-grain mustard, remaining sage and seasoning, then serve with the chicken. Garnish the chicken with fresh sage and serve hot or cold.

Chicken Pastitsio

A traditional Greek pastitsio is a rich, high-fat dish made with ground beef, but this lighter version with chicken is just as tasty.

INGREDIENTS

Serves 4–6

1 pound lean ground chicken
1 large onion, finely chopped
4 tablespoons tomato paste
1 cup red wine or stock
1 teaspoon ground cinnamon
$2^1/2$ cups macaroni
$1^1/4$ cups milk
2 tablespoons margarine
4 tablespoons all-purpose flour
1 teaspoon grated nutmeg
2 tomatoes, sliced
4 tablespoons whole-wheat breadcrumbs
salt and black pepper
green salad, to serve

1 Preheat the oven to 425°F. Fry the ground chicken and chopped onion in a nonstick pan without fat, stirring occasionally until lightly browned.

2 Stir in the tomato paste, red wine and cinnamon. Season, then cover and simmer for 5 minutes, stirring occasionally. Remove from the heat.

3 Cook the macaroni in plenty of boiling, salted water until just tender, then drain.

4 Layer the macaroni with the chicken mixture in a wide ovenproof dish.

5 Place the milk, margarine and flour in a saucepan and whisk over medium heat until thickened and smooth. Add the nutmeg and season to taste.

6 Pour the sauce evenly over the pasta and meat layers. Arrange the tomato slices on top and sprinkle whole-wheat breadcrumbs over the surface.

7 Bake for 30–35 minutes, or until golden brown and bubbling. Serve hot with a fresh green salad.

Crunchy Stuffed Chicken Breasts

These can be prepared ahead of time as long as the stuffing is entirely cold before the chicken is stuffed. It is an ideal dish for entertaining.

INGREDIENTS

Serves 4

4 chicken breasts, boned
2 tablespoons butter
1 garlic clove, crushed
1 tablespoon Dijon mustard

For the stuffing

1 tablespoon butter
1 bunch scallions, sliced
3 tablespoons fresh breadcrumbs
2 tablespoons pine nuts
1 egg yolk
1 tablespoon chopped fresh parsley
salt and black pepper
4 tablespoons grated cheese

For the topping

2 bacon slices, finely chopped
1 cup fresh breadcrumbs
1 tablespoon grated Parmesan cheese
1 tablespoon chopped fresh parsley

1 Preheat the oven to 400°F. To make the stuffing, heat 1 tablespoon of the butter in a frying pan and cook the scallions until soft. Remove from the heat and allow to cool for a few minutes.

2 Add the remaining ingredients and mix thoroughly.

3 To make the topping, fry the chopped bacon until crisp, drain and add to the breadcrumbs, Parmesan cheese and fresh parsley.

4 Carefully cut a deep pocket in each of the chicken breasts, using a sharp knife.

5 Divide the stuffing into fourths and use to fill the pockets. Put in a buttered ovenproof dish.

6 Melt the remaining butter, mix it with the crushed garlic and mustard, and brush liberally over the chicken. Press on the topping and bake uncovered for about 30–40 minutes, or until tender.

Chicken with White Wine and Garlic

Add the extra garlic to this dish if you like a stronger flavor.

INGREDIENTS

Serves 4

1 chicken, 3 1/2 pounds, cut into serving pieces
1 onion, sliced
3–6 garlic cloves, to taste, crushed
1 teaspoon dried thyme
2 cups dry white wine
1 cup green olives (16–18), pitted
1 bay leaf
1 tablespoon lemon juice
1–2 tablespoons butter
salt and black pepper

1 Heat a deep, heavy frying pan. When hot, add the chicken pieces, skin side down, and cook over medium heat until browned, about 10 minutes. Turn and brown the other side, 5–8 minutes more.

2 Transfer the chicken pieces to a plate and set aside.

3 Drain the excess fat from the frying pan, leaving about 1 tablespoon. Add the sliced onion and 1/2 teaspoon salt and cook until just soft, about 5 minutes. Add the garlic and thyme and cook 1 minute more.

4 Add the wine and stir, scraping up any bits that cling to the pan. Bring to a boil and boil for 1 minute. Stir in the olives.

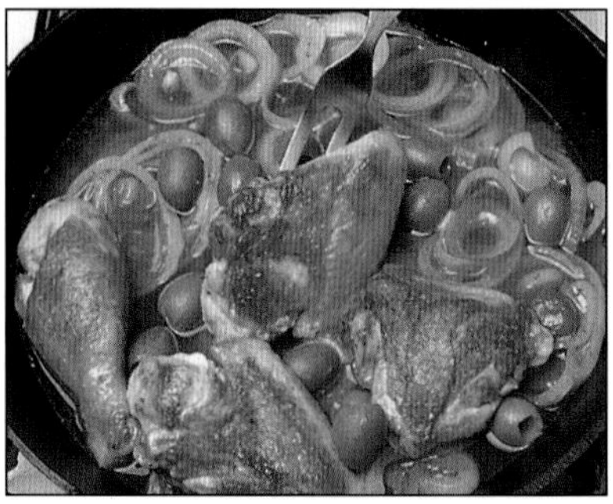

5 Return the chicken pieces to the pan. Add the bay leaf and season lightly with pepper. Lower the heat, cover, and simmer until the chicken is cooked through, about 20–30 minutes.

6 Transfer the chicken pieces to a warmed plate. Stir the lemon juice into the sauce. Whisk in the butter to thicken the sauce slightly. Spoon on top and serve.

Chicken Meat Loaf

Just slice the loaf up and serve it hot or cold.

INGREDIENTS

Serves 4

1 tablespoon olive oil
1 onion, chopped
1 green bell pepper, seeded and chopped
1 garlic clove, crushed
1 pound ground chicken
1 cup fresh breadcrumbs
1 egg, beaten
1/2 cup pine nuts
12 sun-dried tomatoes in oil, drained and chopped
5 tablespoons milk
2 teaspoons chopped fresh rosemary, or 1/2 teaspoon dried rosemary
1 teaspoon ground fennel seeds
1/2 teaspoon dried oregano
1/2 teaspoon salt

1 Preheat the oven to 375°F. Heat the oil in a frying pan. Add the onion, green pepper and garlic and cook over low heat, stirring often, until just softened, about 8–10 minutes. Remove from the heat and allow to cool.

2 Place the chicken in a large bowl. Add the onion mixture and the remaining ingredients and mix thoroughly.

3 Transfer to an 8 1/2 x 4 1/2-inch loaf tin, packing the mixture down firmly. Bake until golden brown, about 1 hour. Serve hot or cold in slices.

Stuffed Chicken Wings

These tasty stuffed wings can be served hot or cold at a buffet. They can be prepared and frozen in advance.

INGREDIENTS

Makes 12

12 large chicken wings

For the filling

1 teaspoon cornstarch
1/4 teaspoon salt
1/2 teaspoon fresh thyme
pinch of black pepper

For the coating

3 cups dried breadcrumbs
2 tablespoons sesame seeds
2 eggs, beaten
oil, for deep-frying

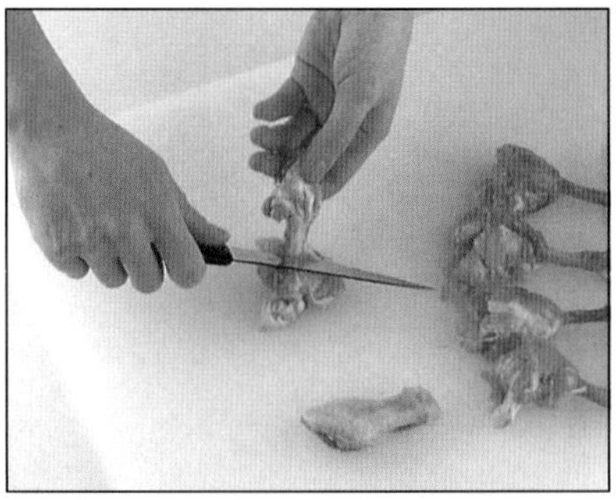

1 Remove the wing tips and discard or use them for making stock. Skin the second joint sections, removing the two small bones, and reserve the meat for the filling.

2 Grind the reserved meat and mix with the filling ingredients.

3 Holding the large end of the bone on the third section of the wing and using a sharp knife, cut the skin and flesh away from the bone, scraping down and pulling the meat over the small end to form a pocket. Repeat this process with the remaining wing sections.

4 Fill the tiny pockets with the filling. Mix the dried breadcrumbs and the sesame seeds together. Place the breadcrumb mixture and the beaten egg in separate dishes.

5 Brush the meat with beaten egg and roll in breadcrumbs to cover. Chill and repeat to make a second layer, forming a thick coating. Chill until ready to fry.

6 Preheat the oven to 350°F. Heat 2 inches of oil in a heavy pan until hot but not smoking, or the breadcrumbs will burn. Gently fry two or three wings at a time until golden brown, remove and drain on paper towels. Complete the cooking in the preheated oven for 15–20 minutes, until tender.

Chicken Paella

There are many variations of this basic recipe. Any seasonal vegetables can be added, together with mussels and other shellfish. Serve right from the pan.

INGREDIENTS

Serves 4

4 chicken legs (thighs and drumsticks)
4 tablespoons olive oil
1 large onion, finely chopped
1 garlic clove, crushed
1 teaspoon ground turmeric
4 ounces chorizo sausage or smoked ham
1 cup long-grain rice
$2^1/2$ cups homemade or canned chicken stock
4 tomatoes, skinned, seeded and chopped
1 red bell pepper, seeded and sliced
1 cup frozen peas
salt and black pepper

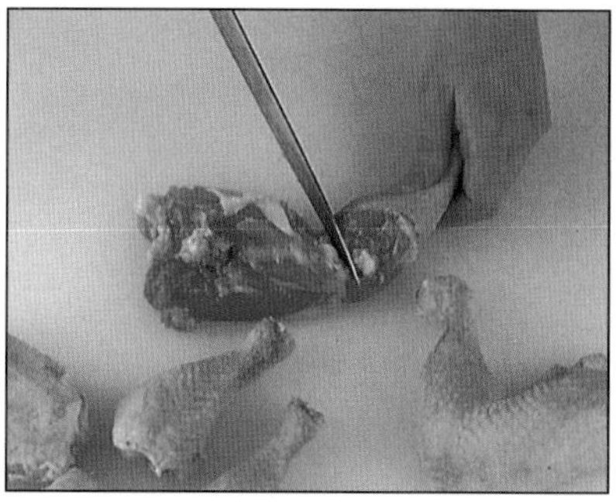

1 Preheat the oven to 350°F. Cut the chicken legs in half.

2 Heat the oil in a 12-inch paella pan or large flameproof casserole and brown the chicken pieces on both sides. Add the onion and garlic and stir in the turmeric. Cook for 2 minutes.

3 Slice the sausage or dice the ham and add to the pan, with the rice and stock. Bring to a boil and season to taste; cover and bake for 15 minutes.

4 Remove from the oven and add the chopped tomatoes, sliced red pepper and frozen peas. Return to the oven and cook for another 10–15 minutes, or until the chicken is tender and the rice has absorbed the stock.

Apricot and Chicken Casserole

A mild curried and fruity chicken dish served with almond rice. Makes a good winter meal.

INGREDIENTS

Serves 4

1 tablespoon oil
8 chicken thighs, boned and skinned
1 medium onion, finely chopped
1 teaspoon medium curry powder
2 tablespoons all-purpose flour
1 7/8 cups homemade or canned chicken stock
juice of 1 large orange
8 dried apricots, halved
1 tablespoon golden raisins
salt and black pepper

For the almond rice

2 cups cooked long-grain rice
1 tablespoon butter
1/2 cup toasted, slivered almonds

1 Preheat the oven to 375°F. Heat the oil in a large frying pan. Cut the chicken into cubes and brown quickly all over in the oil. Add the chopped onion and cook gently until soft and lightly browned.

2 Transfer the chicken and onion to a large flameproof casserole, sprinkle in the curry powder and cook again for a few minutes. Add the flour and blend in the stock and orange juice. Bring to a boil and season with salt and freshly ground black pepper.

3 Add the apricots and golden raisins, cover with a lid and cook gently for an hour, or until tender, in the preheated oven. Adjust the seasoning to taste.

4 To make the almond rice, reheat the pre-cooked rice with the butter and season to taste. Stir in the toasted almonds just before serving.

Stoved Chicken

"Stoved" is derived from the French étouffer *– to cook in a covered pot – and originates from the seventeenth century.*

INGREDIENTS

Serves 4

$2^1/4$ pounds potatoes, cut into $^1/4$-inch slices
2 large onions, thinly sliced
1 tablespoon chopped fresh thyme
2 tablespoons butter
1 tablespoon oil
2 large slices bacon, chopped
4 large chicken quarters, halved
1 bay leaf
$2^1/2$ cups homemade or canned chicken stock
salt and black pepper

1 Preheat the oven to 300°F. Make a thick layer of half the potato slices in the bottom of a large, heavy casserole, then cover with half the onion. Sprinkle with half the thyme, and salt and pepper.

2 Heat the butter and oil in a large frying pan, then brown the bacon and chicken.

3 Using a slotted spoon, transfer the chicken and bacon to the casserole. Reserve the fat in the pan. Sprinkle the remaining thyme, bay leaf and some seasoning over the chicken, then cover with the remaining onion, followed by a neat layer of overlapping potato slices. Sprinkle with seasoning.

4 Pour the stock into the casserole, brush the potatoes with the reserved fat, then cover tightly and cook in the oven for about 2 hours, until the chicken is tender.

5 Preheat the broiler. Uncover the casserole, place under the broiler and cook until the slices of potato are beginning to brown and crisp. Serve hot.

Salads, Barbecues & Grills

Coronation Chicken

A summer favorite – serve with a crisp green salad.

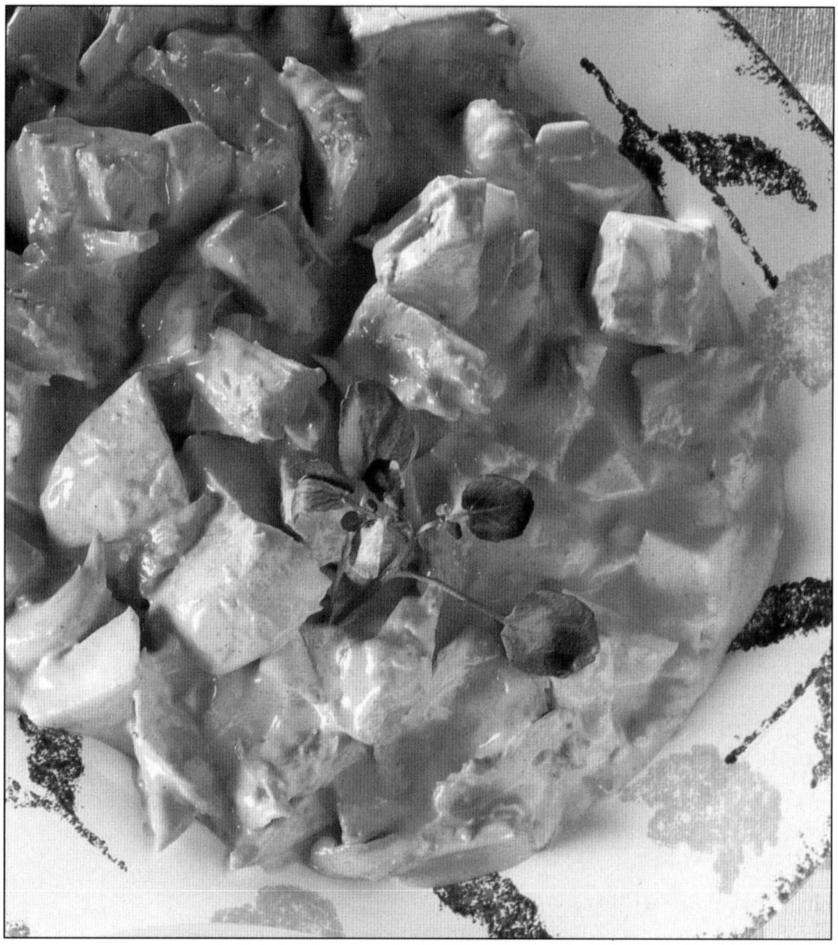

INGREDIENTS

Serves 8

- 1/2 lemon
- 1 chicken, 5–5 1/4 pounds
- 1 onion, quartered
- 1 carrot, quartered
- large bouquet garni
- 8 black peppercorns, crushed
- salt
- watercress sprigs, to garnish

For the sauce

- 1 small onion, chopped
- 1 tablespoon butter
- 1 tablespoon curry paste
- 1 tablespoon tomato paste
- 1/2 cup red wine
- 1 bay leaf
- juice of 1/2 lemon, or more to taste
- 2–3 teaspoons apricot jam
- 1 1/4 cups good-quality mayonnaise
- 1/2 cup whipping cream, whipped
- salt and black pepper

1 Put the lemon half in the chicken cavity, then place the chicken in a saucepan that it just fits. Add the vegetables, bouquet garni, peppercorns and salt.

2 Add enough water to cover two-thirds of the chicken, bring to a boil, then cover and cook gently for 1 1/2 hours, or until the juices run clear.

3 Transfer to a large bowl, pour the cooking liquid over it and let it cool. Skin and bone the chicken, then chop the flesh.

4 To make the sauce, cook the onion in the butter until soft. Add the curry paste, tomato paste, wine, bay leaf and lemon juice, then cook for 10 minutes. Add the apricot jam; sieve and cool.

5 Beat the sauce into the mayonnaise. Fold in the cream; add seasoning, then stir in the chicken and garnish with watercress.

Warm Stir-fried Salad

Warm salads are becoming increasingly popular because they are delicious and nutritious. Arrange the salad leaves on four individual plates, so the hot stir-fry can be served straight from the wok, making sure the lettuce remains crisp and the chicken warm.

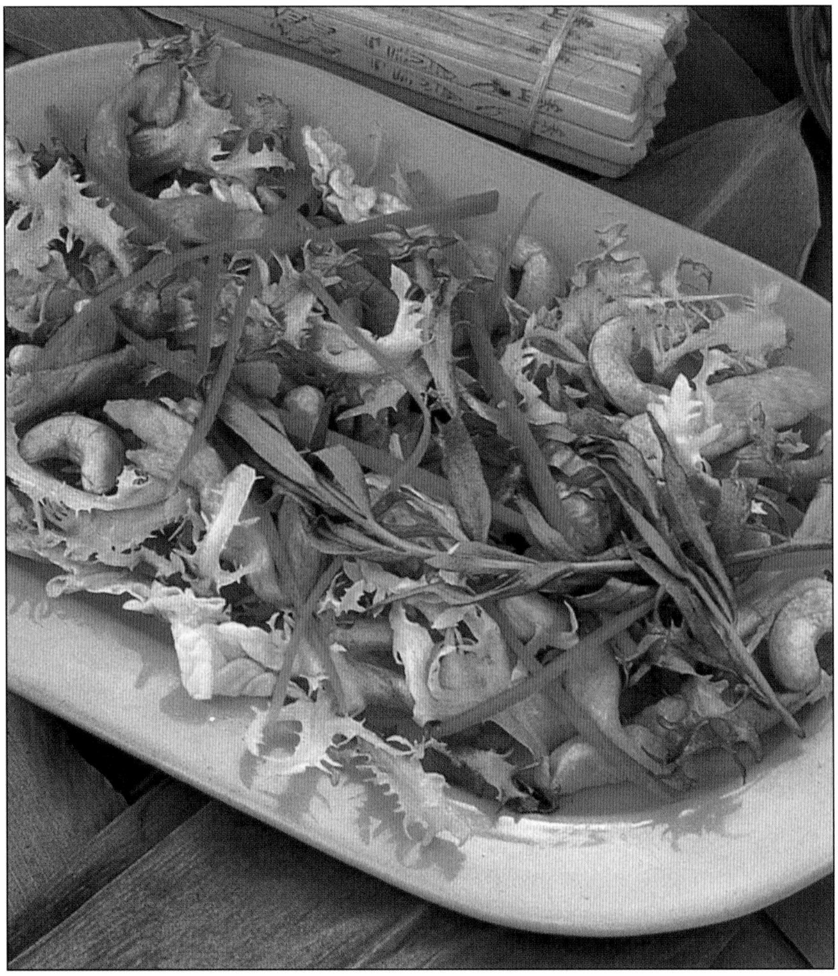

INGREDIENTS

Serves 4

2 chicken breasts, about 8 ounces each, boned and skinned
1 tablespoon chopped fresh tarragon
2-inch piece fresh ginger, peeled and finely chopped
3 tablespoons light soy sauce
1 tablespoon sugar
1 tablespoon sunflower oil
1 head Chinese lettuce
1/2 frisée lettuce or curly endive, torn into bite-size pieces
1 cup unsalted cashews
2 large carrots, peeled and cut into fine strips
salt and black pepper

1 Cut the chicken into fine strips and place in a bowl.

2 To make the marinade, mix together in a bowl the tarragon, ginger, soy sauce, sugar and seasoning.

3 Pour the marinade over the chicken strips and marinate for 2–4 hours.

4 Strain the chicken from the marinade, reserving the liquid. Heat a wok or large frying pan, then add the oil. When the oil is hot, stir-fry the chicken for 3 minutes, add the marinade and simmer for 2–3 minutes.

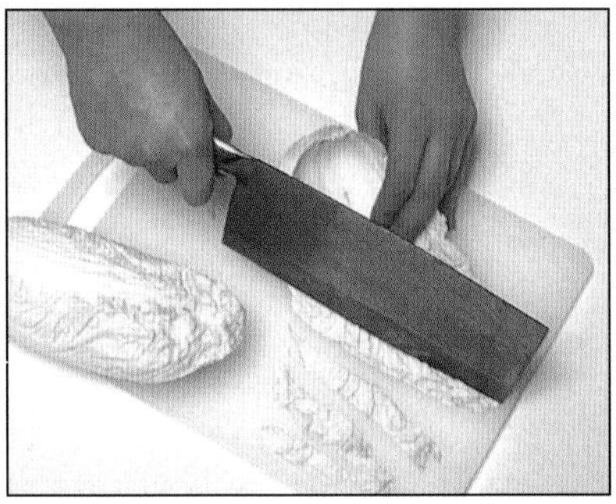

5 Slice the Chinese lettuce and arrange on a plate with the frisée. Toss the cashews and carrots together with the chicken and sauce, pile on top of the bed of lettuce and serve immediately.

Fusilli with Chicken, Tomatoes and Broccoli

This is a really hearty main-course salad for a hungry family.

INGREDIENTS

Serves 4

$1^1/_2$ pounds ripe but firm plum tomatoes, quartered
6 tablespoons olive oil
1 teaspoon dried oregano
salt and black pepper
12 ounces broccoli florets
1 small onion, sliced
1 teaspoon dried thyme
1 pound chicken breasts, boned, skinned and cubed
3 garlic cloves, crushed
1 tablespoon fresh lemon juice
1 pound fusilli

1 Preheat the oven to 400°F.

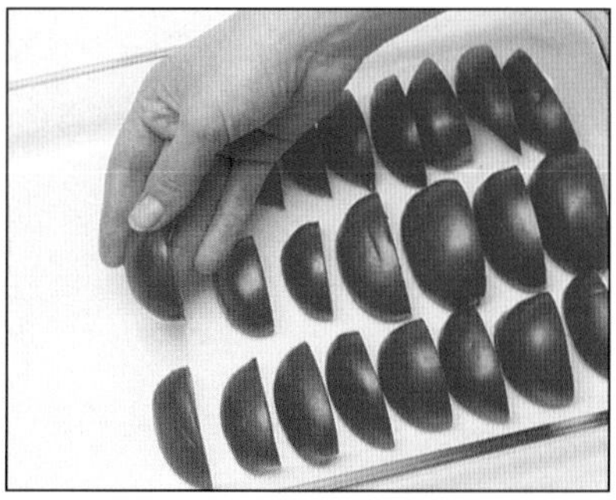

2 Place the tomatoes in a baking dish. Add 1 tablespoon of the oil, the oregano, and $^1/_2$ teaspoon salt and stir to blend.

3 Bake until the tomatoes are just browned, about 30–40 minutes; do not stir.

4 Meanwhile, bring a large pan of salted water to a boil. Add the broccoli and cook until just tender, about 5 minutes. Drain and set aside. (Alternatively, steam the broccoli until tender.)

5 Heat 2 tablespoons of the oil in a large nonstick frying pan. Add the onion, thyme, chicken cubes and $^1/_2$ teaspoon salt. Cook over high heat, stirring until the meat is cooked and beginning to brown, 5–7 minutes. Add the garlic and cook 1 minute more, stirring.

6 Remove from the heat. Stir in the lemon juice and season with pepper. Keep warm until the pasta is cooked.

7 Bring another large pan of salted water to a boil. Add the fusilli and cook until just tender (check the instructions on the package for timing). Drain and place in a large bowl. Toss with the remaining oil.

8 Add the broccoli to the chicken mixture. Add to the fusilli. Add the tomatoes and stir gently to blend. Serve immediately.

Chinese-style Chicken Salad

Shredded chicken is served with a tasty peanut sauce.

INGREDIENTS

Serves 4

4 boneless chicken breasts, about 6 ounces each
4 tablespoons dark soy sauce
pinch of Chinese five-spice powder
a good squeeze of lemon juice
1/2 cucumber, peeled and cut into matchsticks
1 teaspoon salt
3 tablespoons sunflower oil
2 tablespoons sesame oil
1 tablespoon sesame seeds
2 tablespoons dry sherry
2 carrots, cut into matchsticks
8 scallions, shredded
1/2 cup beansprouts

For the sauce

4 tablespoons crunchy peanut butter
2 teaspoons lemon juice
2 teaspoons sesame oil
1/4 teaspoon ground hot chilies
1 scallion, finely chopped

1 Put the chicken pieces into a large pan and just cover with water. Add 1 tablespoon of the soy sauce, the Chinese five-spice powder and lemon juice, cover and bring to a boil, then simmer for about 20 minutes.

2 Place the cucumber matchsticks in a colander, sprinkle with the salt and cover with a weighted plate on top. Let drain for 30 minutes.

3 Heat the oils in a large frying pan or wok. Add the sesame seeds, fry for 30 seconds and then stir in the remaining soy sauce and the sherry. Add the carrots and stir-fry for 2–3 minutes. Remove and reserve.

4 Remove the chicken from the pan and let stand until cool enough to handle. Discard the skins and bash the chicken lightly with a rolling pin to loosen the fibers. Slice in strips and reserve.

5 Rinse the cucumber well, pat dry with paper towels and place in a bowl. Add the scallions, beansprouts, cooked carrots, pan juices and shredded chicken, and mix together. Transfer to a shallow dish. Cover and chill for about 1 hour, turning the mixture in the juices once or twice.

6 To make the sauce, cream the peanut butter with the lemon juice, sesame oil and ground chilies, adding a little hot water to form a paste, then stir in the scallion. Arrange the chicken mixture on a serving dish and serve with the peanut sauce.

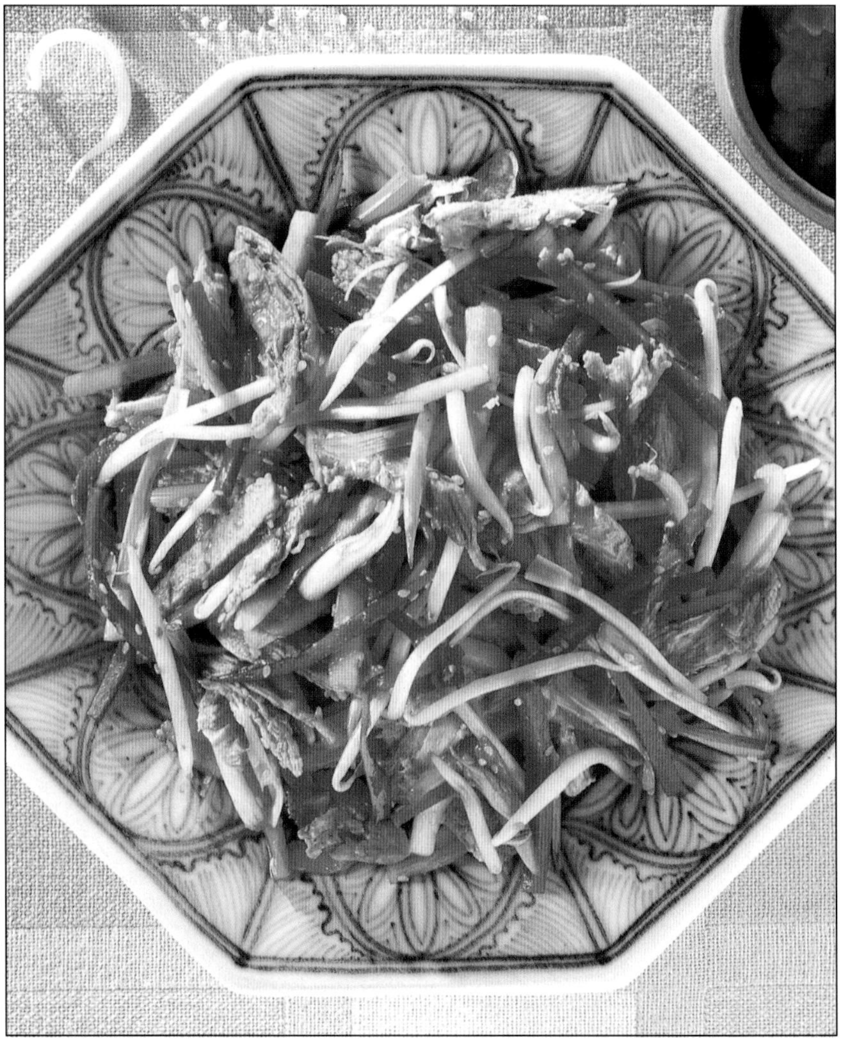

Maryland Salad

Barbecued chicken, corn, bacon, banana and watercress combine here in a sensational main course salad. Serve with baked potatoes and a pat of butter.

INGREDIENTS

Serves 4

4 chicken breasts, boned
8 ounces rindless unsmoked bacon
4 ears corn
3 tablespoons butter, softened
4 ripe bananas, peeled and halved
4 firm tomatoes, halved
1 greenleaf or Boston lettuce
1 bunch watercress
salt and black pepper

For the dressing

5 tablespoons peanut oil
1 tablespoon white wine vinegar
2 teaspoons maple syrup
2 teaspoons mild mustard

1 Season the chicken breasts, brush with oil and barbecue or broil for 15 minutes, turning once. Broil the bacon for 8–10 minutes, or until crisp.

2 Bring a large saucepan of salted water to a boil. Shuck and trim the corn. Boil for 3–5 minutes. For extra flavor, brush with butter and brown over the barbecue or under the broiler. Barbecue or broil the bananas and tomatoes for 6–8 minutes, brushing these with butter too, if you wish.

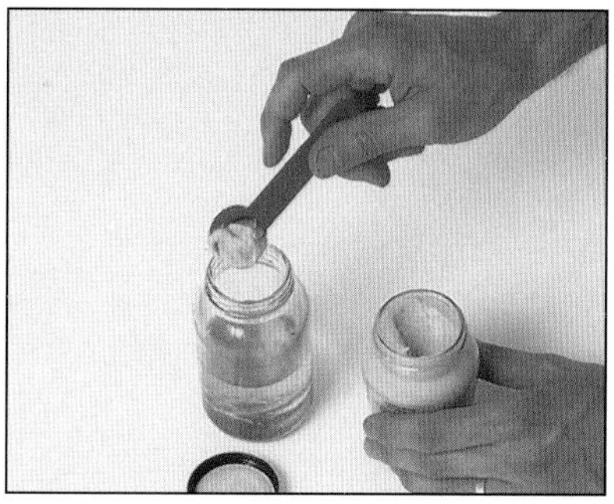

3 To make the dressing, combine the oil, vinegar, maple syrup and mustard with seasoning and 1 tablespoon water in a screw-top jar and shake well.

4 Wash, spin thoroughly and dress the salad leaves.

5 Distribute the salad leaves among 4 large plates. Slice the chicken and arrange over the leaves with the bacon, banana, corn and tomatoes.

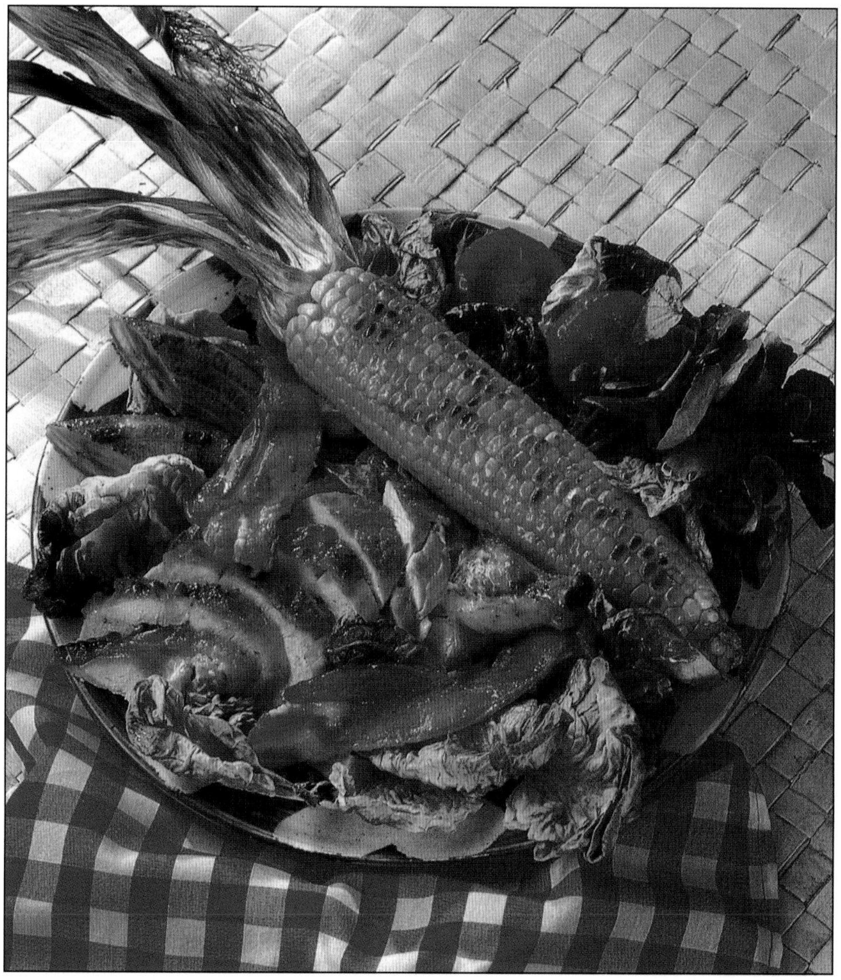

Chicken Liver, Bacon and Tomato Salad

Warm salads are especially welcome during the autumn months when the evenings are growing shorter and cooler. Try this rich salad with sweet spinach and bitter leaves of frisée lettuce.

INGREDIENTS

Serves 4

8 ounces young spinach, stems removed
1 frisée lettuce or curly endive
7 tablespoons peanut or sunflower oil
6 ounces rindless unsmoked bacon, cut into strips
3 ounces day-old bread, crusts removed and cut into short fingers
1 pound chicken livers
4 ounces cherry tomatoes
salt and black pepper

1 Place the salad leaves in a salad bowl. Heat 4 tablespoons of the oil in a large frying pan. Add the bacon and cook for 3–4 minutes, or until crisp and brown. Remove the bacon with a slotted spoon and drain on paper towels.

2 To make the croutons, fry the bread in the bacon-flavored oil, tossing until crisp and golden. Drain on paper towels.

3 Heat the remaining 3 tablespoons oil in the frying pan, add the chicken livers and fry briskly for 2–3 minutes. Pour over the salad leaves, and add the bacon, croutons and tomatoes. Season, toss and serve.

Chicken Satay

Marinate the chicken in the satay sauce overnight to allow the flavors to penetrate it. Soak wooden skewers in water overnight to prevent them from burning while cooking.

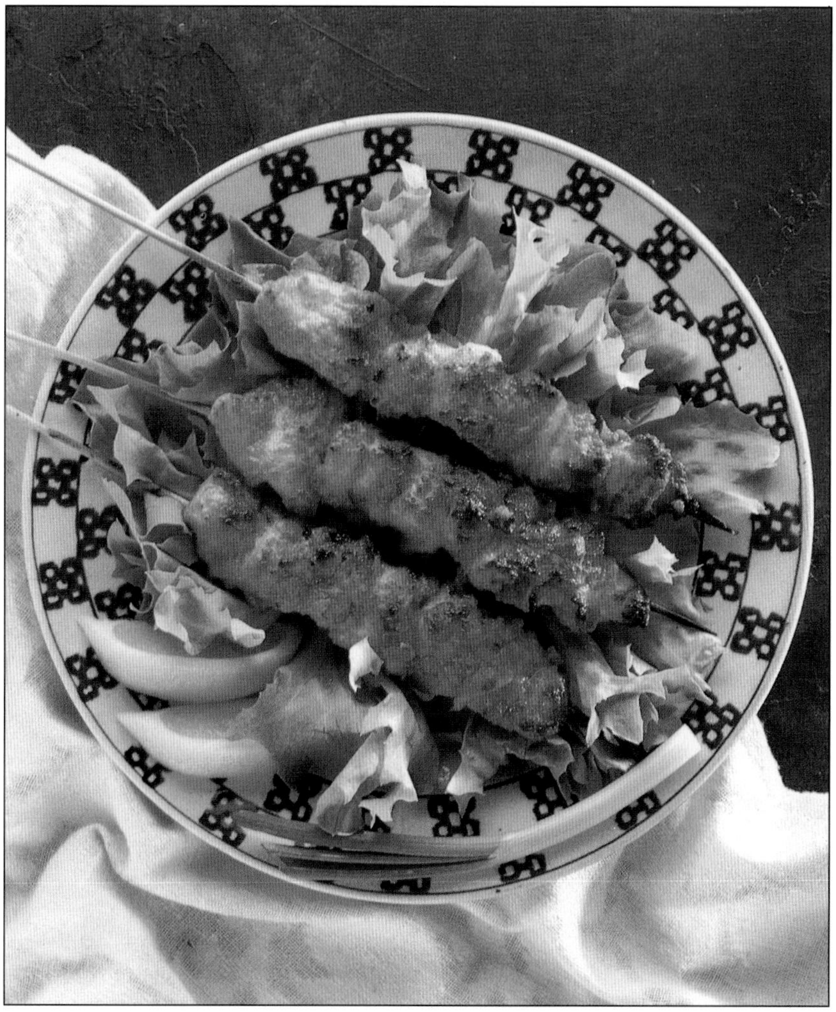

INGREDIENTS

Serves 4

4 chicken breasts
lemon slices, to garnish
lettuce leaves, to serve
scallions, to serve

For the satay

1/2 cup crunchy peanut butter
1 small onion, chopped
1 garlic clove, crushed
2 tablespoons chutney
4 tablespoons olive oil
1 teaspoon light soy sauce
2 tablespoons lemon juice
1/4 teaspoon ground chilies or cayenne pepper

1 Put all the satay ingredients into a food processor or blender and process until smooth. Spoon into a large dish.

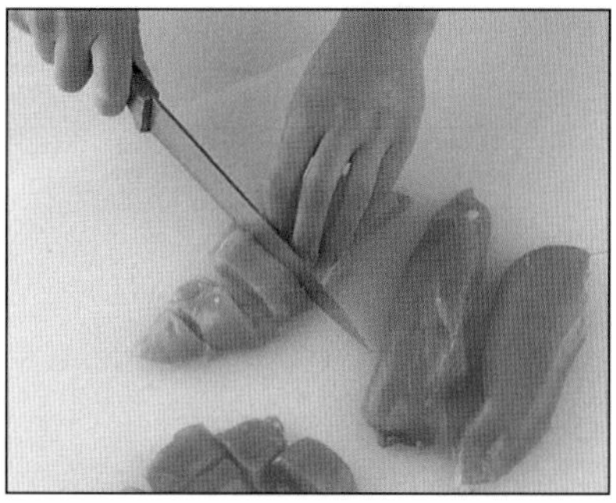

2 Remove all bone and skin from the chicken and cut into 1-inch cubes. Add to the satay mixture and stir to coat the chicken pieces. Cover with plastic wrap and chill for at least 4 hours or, better still, overnight.

3 Preheat the broiler or grill. Thread the chicken pieces onto the wooden skewers.

4 Cook for 10 minutes, brushing occasionally with the satay sauce. Serve on a bed of lettuce and scallions, and garnish with lemon slices.

Minty Yogurt Chicken

Chicken marinated with yogurt, mint, lemon and honey and broiled.

INGREDIENTS

Serves 4

8 chicken thigh portions, skinned
1 tablespoon honey
2 tablespoons lemon (or lime) juice
2 tablespoons plain yogurt
4 tablespoons chopped fresh mint
salt and black pepper
new potatoes and a tomato salad, to serve

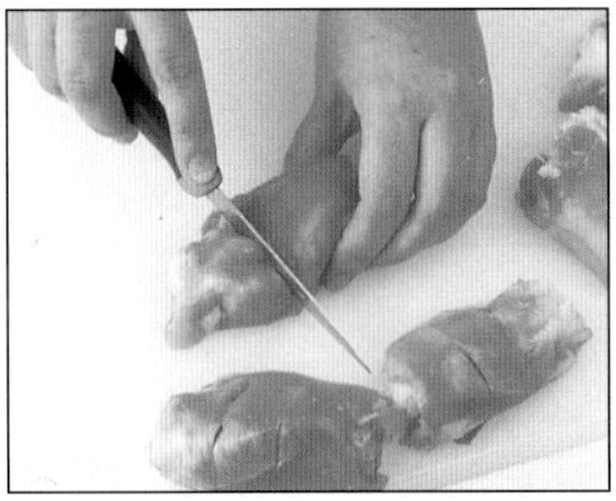

1 Slash the chicken flesh at regular intervals with a sharp knife. Place in a bowl.

2 Mix together the honey, lime or lemon juice, yogurt, seasoning and half the mint.

3 Spoon the marinade over the chicken and let marinate for 30 minutes. Line the broiler pan with foil and cook the chicken under a medium-hot broiler until thoroughly cooked and golden brown, turning the chicken occasionally during cooking.

4 Sprinkle with the remaining mint and serve with the potatoes and tomato salad.

Caribbean Chicken Kebabs

These kebabs have a rich, sunny Caribbean flavor, and the marinade keeps them moist without the need for oil. Serve with a colorful salad and rice.

INGREDIENTS

Serves 4

- $1^1/_4$ pounds chicken breasts, boned and skinned
- finely grated rind of 1 lime
- 2 tablespoons lime juice
- 1 tablespoon rum or sherry
- 1 tablespoon light brown sugar
- 1 teaspoon ground cinnamon
- 2 mangoes, peeled and cubed
- rice and salad, to serve

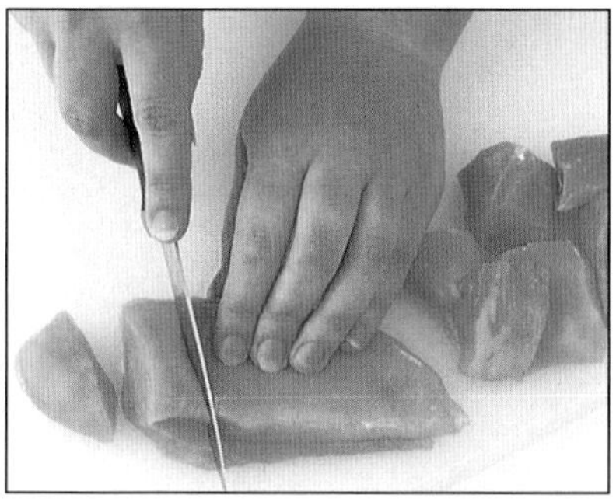

1 Cut the chicken breasts into bite-size chunks and place in a bowl with the grated lime rind and juice, rum or sherry, sugar and cinnamon. Toss well, cover and marinate for 1 hour.

COOK'S TIP

The rum or sherry adds a terrific rich flavor, but it is optional so can be omitted if you prefer to make the dish more economical.

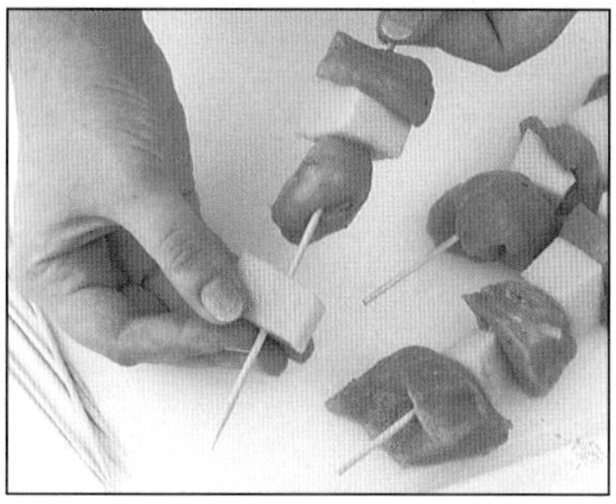

2 Save the juices, and thread the chicken onto four wooden skewers, alternating with the mango cubes.

3 Cook the kebabs under a hot broiler or barbecue for 8–10 minutes, turning occasionally and basting with the reserved juices, until the chicken is tender and golden brown. Serve at once with rice and salad.

Chicken with Pineapple

This chicken has a delicate tang and is very tender. The pineapple not only tenderizes the chicken but also gives it a slight sweetness.

INGREDIENTS

Serves 6

8-ounce can pineapple chunks
1 teaspoon ground cumin
1 teaspoon ground coriander
$\frac{1}{2}$ teaspoon crushed garlic
1 teaspoon ground chilies
1 teaspoon salt
2 tablespoons plain yogurt
1 tablespoon chopped fresh cilantro
orange food coloring (optional)
10 ounces chicken, skinned and boned
$\frac{1}{2}$ red bell pepper
$\frac{1}{2}$ yellow or green bell pepper
1 large onion
6 cherry tomatoes
1 tablespoon vegetable oil

1 Drain the pineapple juice into a bowl. Reserve 8 large chunks of pineapple, squeeze the juice from the remaining chunks into the bowl and set aside. You should have about $\frac{1}{2}$ cup pineapple juice.

2 In a large mixing bowl, blend the cumin, ground coriander, garlic, ground chili, salt, yogurt, fresh cilantro and a few drops of food coloring, if using. Pour the reserved pineapple juice into the mixture and stir.

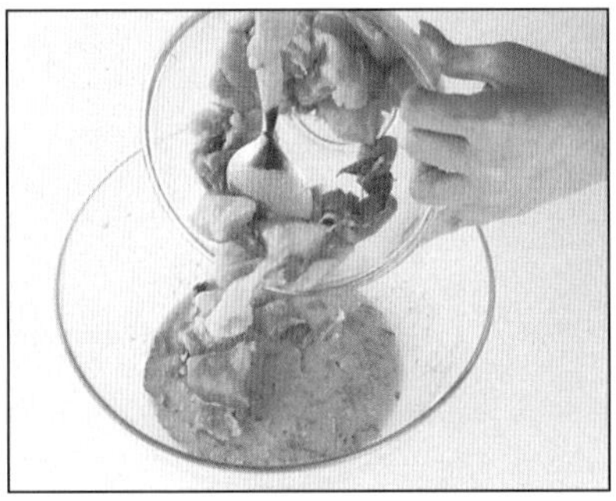

3 Cut the chicken into bite-size cubes, add to the mixing bowl with the yogurt and spice mixture and allow to marinate for about 1–$1\frac{1}{2}$ hours.

4 Cut the peppers and onion into bite-size chunks.

COOK'S TIP

If possible, use a mixture of chicken breast and thigh meat for this recipe.

5 Preheat the broiler to medium. Arrange the chicken pieces, peppers, onion, tomatoes and reserved pineapple chunks alternately on 6 wooden or metal skewers.

6 Baste the kebabs with the oil, then place the skewers on a flameproof dish or broiler pan. Broil, turning and basting the chicken pieces with the marinade regularly, for about 15 minutes.

7 Once the chicken pieces are cooked, remove them from the broiler and serve either with salad or plain boiled rice.

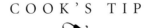

Chicken Breasts with Tomato-Corn Salsa

This hot tomato salsa is good with any broiled or grilled meats.

INGREDIENTS

Serves 4

4 chicken breast halves, about 6 ounces each, boned and skinned
2 tablespoons fresh lemon juice
2 tablespoons olive oil
2 teaspoons ground cumin
2 teaspoons dried oregano
1 tablespoon coarse black pepper
salt

For the salsa

1 fresh hot green chili pepper
1 pound tomatoes, seeded and chopped
$1^1/4$ cups corn, freshly cooked or thawed
3 scallions, chopped
1 tablespoon chopped fresh parsley
2 tablespoons chopped fresh cilantro
2 tablespoons fresh lemon juice
3 tablespoons olive oil
1 teaspoon salt

1 With a mallet, pound the chicken breasts between two sheets of plastic wrap until thin.

2 In a shallow dish, combine the lemon juice, oil, cumin, oregano and pepper.

3 Add the chicken and turn to coat. Cover and let stand for at least 2 hours, or chill overnight.

4 To make the salsa, char the chili skin over a gas flame (or under the broiler.) Let cool for 5 minutes. Wearing rubber gloves, carefully rub off the charred skin. For a less hot flavor, discard the seeds.

5 Chop the chili very finely and place in a bowl. Add the rest of the salsa ingredients and mix well.

6 Remove the chicken from the marinade. Season lightly.

7 Heat a ridged broiler pan. Add the chicken breasts and cook until browned, about 3 minutes. Turn and cook the meat on the other side for 3–4 minutes more. Serve the chicken with the salsa.

Barbecued Jerk Chicken

Jerk refers to the blend of herb and spice seasoning rubbed into meat before it is roasted over charcoal sprinkled with pimiento berries. In Jamaica, jerk seasoning was originally used only for pork, but jerked chicken is equally good.

INGREDIENTS

Serves 4

8 chicken pieces

For the marinade

1 teaspoon ground allspice
1 teaspoon ground cinnamon
1 teaspoon dried thyme
1/4 teaspoon freshly grated nutmeg
2 teaspoons raw sugar
2 garlic cloves, crushed
1 tablespoon finely chopped onion
1 tablespoon chopped scallion
1 tablespoon vinegar
2 tablespoons peanut oil
1 tablespoon lime juice
1 hot chili pepper, chopped
salt and black pepper
lettuce leaves, to serve

1 Combine all the marinade ingredients in a small bowl. Using a fork, mash them together well to form a thick paste.

2 Lay the chicken pieces on a plate or board and make several lengthwise slits in the flesh. Rub the seasoning all over the chicken and into the slits.

3 Place the chicken pieces in a dish, cover with plastic wrap and marinate overnight in the fridge. Shake off any excess seasoning from the chicken. Brush with oil and place either on a baking sheet or a barbecue grill, if barbecuing.

4 Cook under a preheated broiler for 45 minutes, turning often. Or, if barbecuing, light the coals and when ready, cook over the coals for 30 minutes, turning often. Serve hot with lettuce leaves.

COOK'S TIP

The flavor is best if you marinate the chicken overnight.

Grilled Chicken

The flavor of this dish, known in Indonesia as Ayam Bakur, *will be more intense if the chicken is marinated overnight. It is an ideal recipe for a party, because the final broiling, barbecuing or baking can be done at the last minute.*

INGREDIENTS

Serves 4

1 chicken, 3–3 1/2 pounds
4 garlic cloves, crushed
2 lemon grass stems, lower 2 inches sliced
1 teaspoon ground turmeric
2 cups water
3–4 bay leaves
3 tablespoons each dark and light soy sauce
1/4 cup butter or margarine
salt
boiled rice, to serve

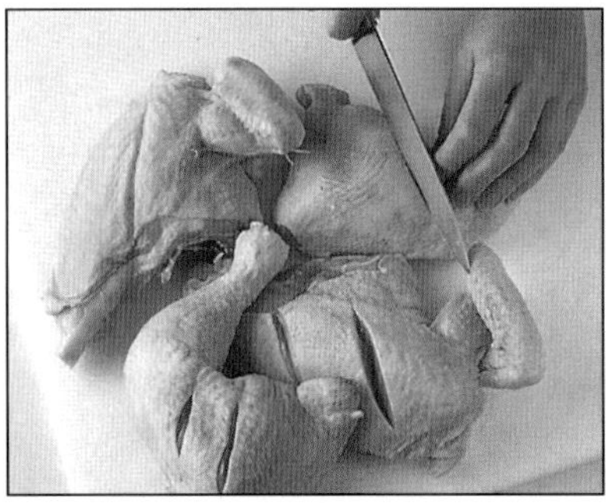

1 Cut the chicken into 4 or 8 portions. Slash the fleshy part of each portion twice and set aside.

2 Grind the garlic, sliced lemon grass, turmeric and salt together into a paste in a food processor or with a mortar and pestle. Rub the paste into the chicken pieces and leave for at least 30 minutes. Wear rubber gloves for this, as the turmeric will stain; or wash your hands immediately after mixing, if you prefer.

3 Transfer the chicken to a wok and pour in the water. Add the bay leaves and bring to a boil. Cover and cook gently for 30 minutes, adding a little more water, if necessary, and stirring occasionally.

4 Just before serving, add the two soy sauces to the pan together with the butter or margarine.

5 Cook until the chicken is well-coated and the sauce has almost been absorbed. Transfer the chicken to a preheated broiler or barbecue, or an oven preheated to 400°F, to complete the cooking. Cook for another 10–15 minutes, turning the pieces often so they become golden brown all over. Take care not to let them burn. Baste with remaining sauce during cooking. Serve with boiled rice.

Mediterranean Chicken Skewers

These skewers are easy to assemble, and can be cooked under the broiler or on a charcoal grill.

INGREDIENTS

Serves 4

6 tablespoons olive oil
3 tablespoons fresh lemon juice
1 clove garlic, finely chopped
2 tablespoons chopped fresh basil
2 medium zucchini
1 long thin eggplant
11 ounces boneless chicken, cut into 2-inch cubes
12–16 pickled onions
1 bell pepper, red or yellow, cut into 2-inch squares
salt and black pepper

1 In a small bowl, mix the oil with the lemon juice, garlic and basil. Season with salt and pepper.

2 Slice the zucchini and eggplant lengthwise into strips 1/4-inch thick. Cut them horizontally about two-thirds of the way along their length. Discard the shorter length. Wrap half the chicken pieces with the zucchini slices, and the other half with the eggplant slices.

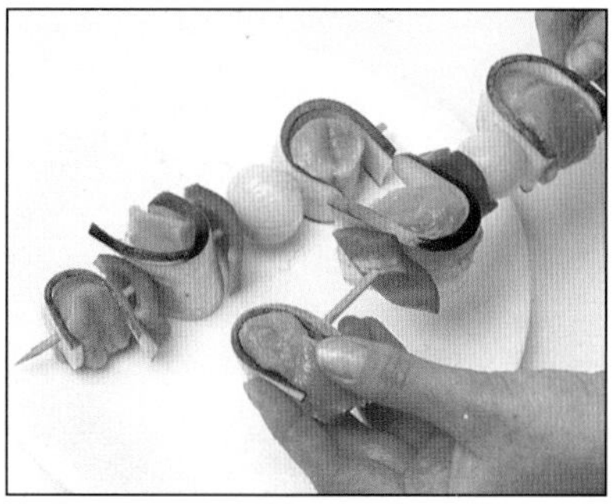

3 Prepare the skewers by alternating the chicken, onions and pepper pieces. Lay the prepared skewers on a platter, and sprinkle with the flavored oil. Let marinate for at least 30 minutes. Preheat the broiler, or prepare a charcoal grill.

4 Broil or grill for about 10 minutes, or until the vegetables are tender, turning the skewers occasionally. Serve hot.

Roasts & Pies

Traditional Roast Chicken

Serve with bacon rolls, small sausages, gravy and stuffing balls.

INGREDIENTS

Serves 4

1 chicken, about 4 pounds
lean bacon strips
2 tablespoons butter
salt and black pepper

For the prune and nut stuffing

2 tablespoons butter
1/2 cup chopped pitted prunes
1/2 cup chopped walnuts
1 cup fresh breadcrumbs
1 egg, beaten
1 tablespoon chopped fresh parsley
1 tablespoon chopped fresh chives
2 tablespoons sherry or Port

For the gravy

2 tablespoons all-purpose flour
1 1/4 cups homemade or canned chicken stock

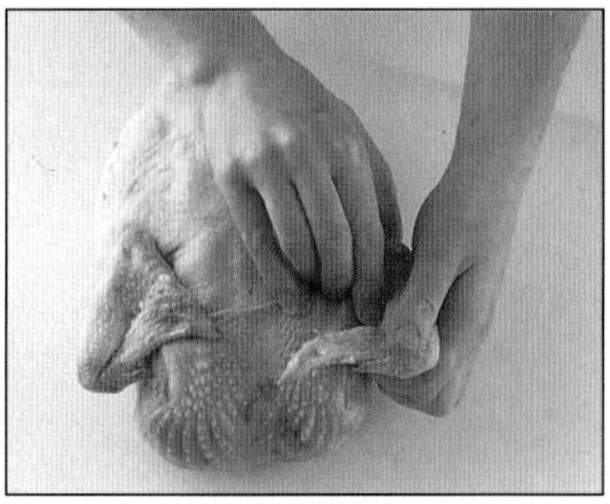

1 Preheat the oven to 375°F. Mix all the stuffing ingredients in a bowl and season well with salt and pepper.

2 Stuff the neck end of the chicken quite loosely, allowing room for the breadcrumbs to swell during cooking. (Any remaining stuffing can be shaped into balls and fried to accompany the roast.)

3 Tuck the neck skin under the bird to secure the stuffing and hold in place with the wing tips, or sew with strong thread or fine string.

4 Place in a roasting pan and cover the breast with the bacon strips. Spread with the remaining butter, cover loosely with foil and roast for about 1 1/2 hours. Baste with the juices in the roasting pan 3 or 4 times during cooking.

5 Remove any trussing string, transfer to a serving plate, cover with foil and let stand while making the gravy. (This standing time allows the flesh to relax and makes carving easier.)

6 Spoon off the fat from the juices in the pan. Blend in the flour and cook gently until golden brown. Add the stock and bring to a boil, stirring until thickened. Adjust the seasoning and strain into a sauceboat to serve.

Roast Chicken with Fennel

In Italy this dish is prepared with wild fennel. Cultivated fennel bulb works just as well.

INGREDIENTS

Serves 4–5

1 roasting chicken, about 3 1/2 pounds
1 onion, quartered
1/2 cup olive oil
2 medium fennel bulbs
1 clove garlic, peeled
pinch of grated nutmeg
3–4 thin slices pancetta or bacon
1/2 cup dry white wine
salt and black pepper

1 Preheat the oven to 350°F. Sprinkle the chicken cavity with salt and pepper. Place the onion quarters in the cavity. Rub the chicken with about 3 tablespoons of the olive oil. Place in a roasting pan.

2 Cut the green fronds from the tops of the fennel bulbs. Chop the fronds together with the garlic. Place in a small bowl and mix with the nutmeg and seasoning.

3 Sprinkle the fennel mixture over the chicken, pressing it on the oiled skin. Cover the breast with the slices of pancetta or bacon. Sprinkle with 2 tablespoons of the oil. Place in the oven and roast for 30 minutes.

4 Meanwhile, boil or steam the fennel bulbs until barely tender. Remove from the heat and cut into quarters or sixths lengthwise. After the chicken has been cooking for 30 minutes, remove the pan from the oven. Baste the chicken with any oils in the pan.

5 Arrange the fennel pieces around the chicken. Sprinkle the fennel with the remaining oil. Pour about half the wine on the chicken, and return to the oven.

6 After 30 minutes more, baste the chicken again. Pour on the remaining wine. Cook for 15–20 minutes. To test, prick the thigh with a fork. If the juices run clear, the chicken is cooked. Serve the chicken surrounded by the fennel.

Chicken with Ham and Cheese

This tasty combination comes from Emilia-Romagna, where it is also prepared with veal.

INGREDIENTS

Serves 4

4 small chicken breasts, skinned and boned
flour seasoned with salt and freshly ground black pepper, for dredging
4 tablespoons butter
3–4 leaves fresh sage
4 thin slices prosciutto or ham, cut in half
1/2 cup freshly grated Parmesan cheese

1 Cut each breast in half lengthwise to make two flat fillets of approximately the same thickness. Dredge the chicken in the seasoned flour, and shake off the excess.

2 Preheat the broiler. Heat the butter in a large heavy frying pan and add the sage leaves. Add the chicken, in one layer, and cook over low to medium heat until golden brown on both sides, turning as necessary. This will take about 15 minutes.

3 Remove the chicken from the heat, and arrange on a flameproof serving dish or broiler pan. Place one piece of ham on each chicken fillet and top with the grated Parmesan. Broil for 3–4 minutes, or until the cheese has melted. Serve at once.

Pot Roast Chicken with Sausage Stuffing

These casseroled chickens will be tender and succulent.

INGREDIENTS

Serves 6

2 chickens, $2^1/2$ pounds each
2 tablespoons vegetable oil
$1^1/2$ cups homemade or canned chicken stock or half wine and half stock
1 bay leaf

For the stuffing

1 pound sausage
1 small onion, chopped
1–2 garlic cloves, finely chopped
1 teaspoon hot paprika
$^1/2$ teaspoon dried chili (optional)
$^1/2$ teaspoon dried thyme
$^1/4$ teaspoon ground allspice
1 cup coarse fresh breadcrumbs
1 egg, beaten to mix
salt and black pepper

1 Preheat the oven to 350°F.

2 For the stuffing, put the sausage, onion and garlic in a frying pan and fry over medium heat until the sausage is lightly browned and crumbly, stirring and turning so it cooks evenly. Remove from the heat and mix in the remaining stuffing ingredients with salt and pepper to taste.

3 Divide the stuffing between the chickens, packing it into the body cavities (or, if preferred, stuff the neck end and bake the leftover stuffing in a separate dish). Truss the birds.

4 Heat the oil in a flameproof casserole just big enough to hold the chickens. Brown the birds all over.

5 Add the stock and bay leaf and season. Cover and bring to a boil, then transfer to the oven. Roast, covered, for $1^1/4$ hours or until the birds are cooked (the juices will run clear).

6 Untruss the chickens and spoon the stuffing onto a serving platter. Arrange the birds and serve with the strained cooking liquid.

VARIATION

For Pot Roast Guinea Hens, use 2 guinea hens instead of chickens.

Rock Cornish Hens Waldorf

Sunday roast and stuffing, with a difference.

INGREDIENTS

Serves 6

6 Rock Cornish hens, about $1^1/_4$ pounds each
salt and black pepper
3–4 tablespoons butter or margarine melted

For the stuffing

2 tablespoons butter
1 onion, finely chopped
$2^1/_4$ cups cooked rice
2 celery stalks, finely chopped
2 red apples, cored and finely diced
$^1/_3$ cup walnuts, chopped
5 tablespoons cream sherry or apple juice
2 tablespoons lemon juice

1 Preheat the oven to 350°F. To make the stuffing, melt the butter in a small frying pan and fry the onion, stirring occasionally, until soft. Pour the onion and butter into a bowl and add the remaining stuffing ingredients. Season with salt and pepper and mix well.

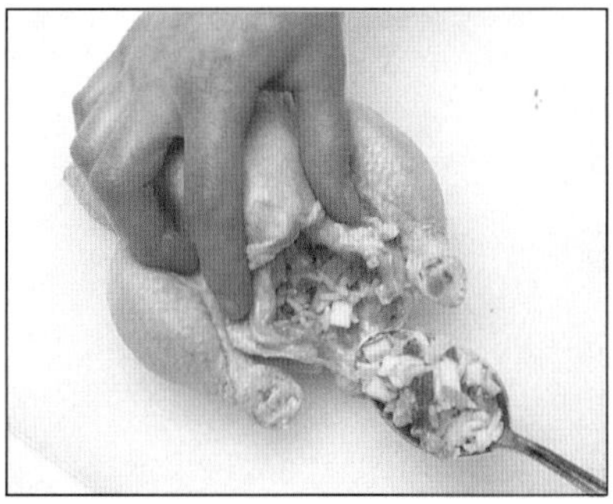

2 Divide the stuffing among the birds, stuffing the body cavities. Truss the birds and arrange in a roasting pan. Sprinkle with salt and pepper and drizzle on the melted butter.

3 Roast for about $1^1/_4$–$1^1/_2$ hours. Untruss before serving.

CARVING POULTRY

Carving a bird neatly for serving makes the presentation attractive. You will need a sharp long-bladed knife, or an electric knife, plus a long 2-pronged fork and a carving board with a groove around the border to catch the juices.

Cut away any trussing string. For a stuffed bird, spoon the stuffing from the cavity into a serving dish. For easier carving, remove the wishbone.

Insert the fork into one breast to hold the bird steady. Cut through the skin to the ball and socket joint on that side of the body, then slice through it to sever the leg from the body. Repeat on the other side.

1 Slice through the ball and socket joint in each leg to sever the thigh and drumstick. If carving turkey, slice the meat off the thigh and drumstick, parallel to the bone, turning to get even slices; leave chicken thighs and drumsticks whole.

2 To carve the breast of a turkey or chicken, cut $^1/_4$-inch thick slices at an angle, slicing down on both sides of the breastbone. For smaller birds, remove the meat on each side of the breastbone in a single piece, then slice across.

Chicken, Leek and Parsley Pie

The flavors of chicken and leek complement each other wonderfully.

INGREDIENTS

Serves 4–6

For the pastry

$2^1/_2$ cups all-purpose flour
pinch of salt
scant 1 cup butter, diced
2 egg yolks

For the filling

3 partly boned chicken breasts
flavoring ingredients, such as bouquet garni, black peppercorns, onion and carrot
4 tablespoons butter
2 leeks, thinly sliced
$^1/_2$ cup grated Cheddar cheese
$^1/_3$ cup finely grated Parmesan cheese
3 tablespoons chopped fresh parsley
2 tablespoons whole-grain mustard
1 teaspoon cornstarch
$1^1/_4$ cups heavy cream
salt and black pepper
beaten egg, to glaze
mixed green salad, to serve

1 To make the pastry, first sift the flour and salt. Blend the butter and egg yolks in a food processor until creamy. Add the flour and process until the mixture is just coming together. Add about 1 tablespoon cold water and process for a few seconds more. Turn out onto a lightly floured surface and knead lightly. Wrap in plastic and chill for about 1 hour.

2 Meanwhile, poach the chicken breasts in water to cover, with the flavoring ingredients added. Cook the chicken until tender. Let cool in the liquid.

3 Preheat the oven to 400°F. Divide the pastry into two pieces, one slightly larger than the other. Roll out the larger piece on a lightly floured surface and use to line a 7 x 11-inch baking dish or pan. Prick the base with a fork and bake for 15 minutes. Set aside to cool.

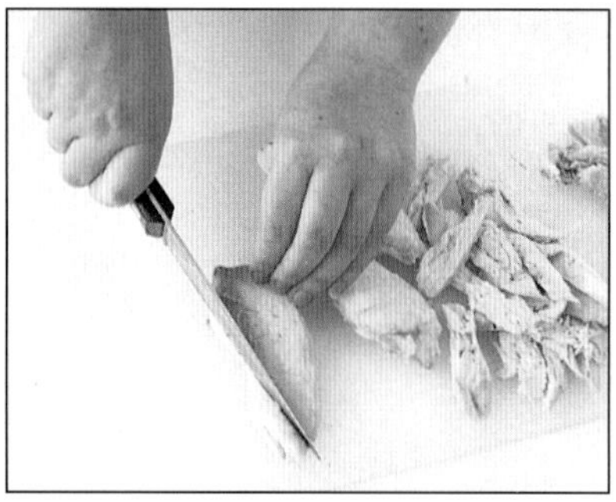

4 Lift the cooled chicken from the poaching liquid and discard the skins and bones. Cut the chicken into strips. Set aside.

5 Melt the butter in a frying pan and fry the sliced leeks over low heat, stirring occasionally, until soft.

6 Stir in the Cheddar, Parmesan and chopped parsley. Spread half the leek mixture over the cooked pastry shell, leaving a border all the way around.

7 Cover the leek mixture with the chicken strips, then top with the remaining leek mixture. Mix together the whole-grain mustard, cornstarch and cream in a small bowl. Add seasoning to taste. Pour the mixture over the chicken and leek filling.

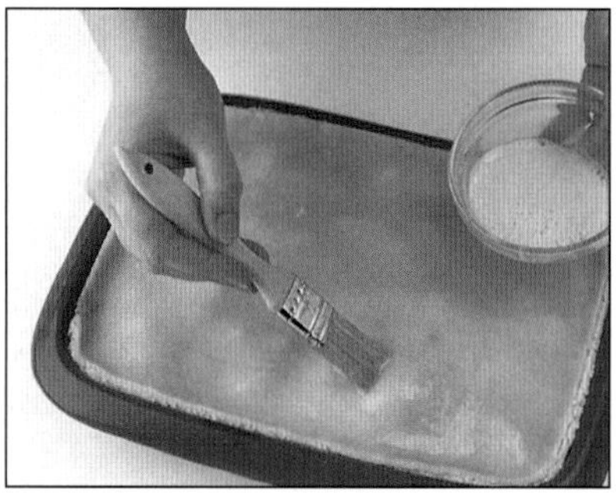

8 Moisten the edges of the cooked pastry shell. Roll out the remaining pastry into a rectangle and use to cover the pie. Brush the top of the pie with beaten egg and bake in the preheated oven for 30–40 minutes, or until the pie is golden and crisp. Serve hot, cut into generous portions, with a mixed green salad.

Curried Chicken and Apricot Pie

This sweet and sour pie is unusually enticing. Use boneless turkey instead of chicken, if you wish.

INGREDIENTS

Serves 6

2 tablespoons sunflower oil
1 large onion, chopped
1 pound chicken, boned and roughly chopped
1 tablespoon curry paste or powder
2 tablespoons apricot or peach chutney
1/2 cup dried apricots, halved
4 ounces cooked carrots, sliced
1 teaspoon mixed dried herbs
4 tablespoons crème fraîche or sour cream
12 ounces ready-made shortcrust pastry
a little egg or milk, to glaze
salt and black pepper

1 Heat the oil in a large pan and fry the onion and chicken until lightly browned. Add the curry paste or powder and fry for another 2 minutes.

2 Add the chutney, apricots, carrots, herbs and crème fraîche to the pan with seasoning. Mix well and then transfer to a deep 5-cup pie dish.

3 Roll out the pastry to 1 inch wider than the pie dish. Cut a strip of pastry from the edge. Damp the rim of the dish, press on the strip, then brush with water and place the sheet of pastry on top, pressing to seal.

4 Preheat the oven to 375°F. Trim any excess pastry and use it to make an attractive pattern on the top, if you wish. Brush all over with beaten egg or milk and bake for 40 minutes, until crisp and golden.

Farmhouse Flan

The lattice pastry topping makes this flan look extra special.

INGREDIENTS

Serves 4

2 cups whole wheat flour
1/4 cup butter, cubed
1/3 cup crisco or vegetable shortening
1 teaspoon caraway seeds
1 tablespoon oil
1 onion, chopped
1 garlic clove, crushed
2 cups chopped cooked chicken
1 1/2 cups watercress leaves, chopped
grated rind of 1/2 small lemon
2 eggs, lightly beaten
3/4 cup heavy or whipping cream
3 tablespoons plain yogurt
a good pinch of grated nutmeg
3 tablespoons grated Caerphilly or Cheddar cheese
beaten egg, to glaze
salt and black pepper

1 Place the flour in a bowl with a pinch of salt. Add the butter and shortening and rub into the flour with your fingertips until the mixture resembles breadcrumbs. (Alternatively, you can use a blender or food processor for this.)

2 Stir in the caraway seeds and 3 tablespoons icewater and mix to a firm dough. Knead lightly on a floured surface until smooth.

3 Roll out the pastry and use to line a 7 x 11-inch quiche pan. Reserve the trimmings. Prick the bottom and chill for at least 20 minutes. Place a baking sheet in the oven and preheat it to 400°F.

4 Heat the oil in a frying pan and sauté the onion and garlic for 5–8 minutes, until just softened. Remove from the heat and cool.

5 Line the pastry shell with waxed paper and fill with dried beans. Bake for 10 minutes, then remove the paper and beans and cook for 5 minutes.

6 Mix the onion, garlic, chicken, watercress and lemon rind. Spoon into the pastry shell. Beat the eggs, cream, yogurt, nutmeg, cheese and seasoning and pour. Roll out the pastry trimmings and cut out 1/2-inch strips. Brush with egg, then lay in a lattice pattern over the flan. Press the ends onto the pastry edge. Bake for 35 minutes, or until the top is golden. Serve warm or cold.

Chicken and Mushroom Pie

Use a mixture of dried and fresh mushrooms for this pie.

INGREDIENTS

Serves 6

1/4 cup dried porcini mushrooms
4 tablespoons butter
2 tablespoons all-purpose flour
1 cup chicken stock, warmed
1/4 cup whipping cream or milk
1 onion, coarsely chopped
2 carrots, sliced
2 stalks celery, coarsely chopped
3/4 cup fresh mushrooms, quartered
3 cups cooked chicken meat, cubed
1/2 cup fresh or frozen peas
salt and black pepper
beaten egg, for glazing

For the crust

2 cups all-purpose flour
1/4 teaspoon salt
1/2 cup cold butter, cut into pieces
1/3 cup crisco or vegetable shortening
4–8 tablespoons icewater

1 To make the crust, sift the flour and salt into a bowl. Cut in the butter and shortening until the mixture resembles breadcrumbs. Sprinkle with 6 tablespoons icewater and mix until the dough holds together. Add a little more water, 1 tablespoon at a time if necessary.

2 Gather the dough into a ball and flatten into a disk. Wrap in waxed paper and chill at least 30 minutes.

3 Place the porcini mushrooms in a small bowl. Add hot water to cover and soak until soft, about 30 minutes. Lift out of the water with a slotted spoon, to leave any grit behind, and drain. Discard the soaking water.

4 Preheat the oven to 375°F.

5 Melt 2 tablespoons of the butter in a heavy saucepan. Whisk in the flour and cook until bubbling, whisking constantly. Add the warm stock and cook over medium heat, whisking, until the mixture boils. Cook 2–3 minutes more. Whisk in the cream or milk. Season with salt and pepper. Put to one side.

6 Heat the remaining butter in a large nonstick frying pan until foamy. Add the onion and carrots and cook until softened, about 5 minutes. Add the celery and fresh mushrooms and cook 5 minutes more. Stir in the chicken, peas, and drained porcini mushrooms.

7 Add the chicken mixture to the sauce and stir. Taste for seasoning. Transfer to a rectangular 10-cup baking dish.

8 Roll out the dough to about 1/8 inch thick. Cut out a rectangle about 1 inch larger all around than the dish. Lay the rectangle of dough over the filling. Make a decorative crimped edge by pushing the index finger of one hand between the thumb and index finger of the other.

9 Cut several vents in the top crust to allow steam to escape. Brush with the egg to glaze.

10 Press together the dough trimmings, then roll out again. Cut into strips and lay them over the top crust. Glaze again. If desired, roll small balls of dough and set them in the "windows" in the lattice.

11 Bake until the top crust is browned, about 30 minutes. Serve the pie hot.

Hot & Spicy

Cajun Chicken

Use ham and shrimp if you have them, but chicken and chorizo sausage are the main ingredients for this dish.

INGREDIENTS

Serves 4

1 chicken, 2 1/2 pounds
1 1/2 onions
1 bay leaf
4 black peppercorns
1 parsley sprig
2 tablespoons vegetable oil
2 garlic cloves, chopped
1 green bell pepper, seeded and chopped
1 stalk celery, chopped
1 1/4 cups long-grain rice
1 cup chorizo sausage, sliced
1 cup chopped cooked ham
14-ounce can chopped tomatoes with herbs
1/2 teaspoon ground chilies
1/2 teaspoon cumin seeds
1/2 teaspoon ground cumin
1 teaspoon dried thyme
1 cup cooked peeled shrimp
dash of Tabasco sauce
chopped parsley, to garnish

1 Place the chicken in a large flameproof casserole and add 2 1/2 cups cold water. Add the half onion, the bay leaf, peppercorns and parsley and bring to a boil. Cover and simmer gently for about 1 1/2 hours.

2 When the chicken is cooked, lift it out of the stock, remove the skin and carcass and chop the meat. Strain the stock, allow to cool and reserve.

3 Chop the remaining onion and heat the oil in a large frying pan. Add the onion, garlic, green pepper and celery. Fry for about 5 minutes, then stir in the rice, coating the grains with the oil. Add the sausage, ham and reserved chopped chicken and fry for another 2–3 minutes, stirring frequently.

4 Pour in the tomatoes and 1 1/4 cups of the reserved stock and add the ground chilies, cumin and thyme. Bring to a boil, then cover and simmer gently for 20 minutes, or until the rice is tender and the liquid is absorbed.

5 Stir in the shrimp and Tabasco. Cook for another 5 minutes, then season well and serve hot, garnished with chopped parsley.

Butterflied Deviled Game Hens

Butterfly *describes very well the idea, if not the actual shape of birds that are split and skewered flat for cooking.*

INGREDIENTS

Serves 4

1 tablespoon powdered English mustard
1 tablespoon paprika
1 tablespoon ground cumin
4 teaspoons ketchup
1 tablespoon lemon juice
5 tablespoons butter, melted
4 Rock Cornish hens, about 1 pound each
salt

1 Combine the mustard, paprika, cumin, ketchup, lemon juice and salt until smooth, then gradually stir in the butter.

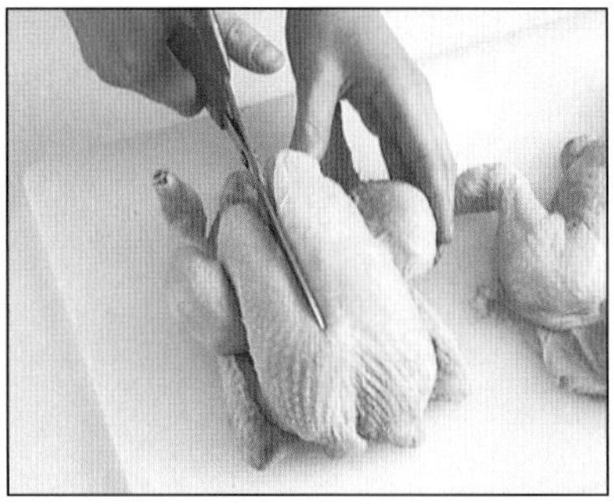

2 Using game shears or strong kitchen scissors, split each bird along one side of the backbone, then cut down the other side of the backbone to remove it.

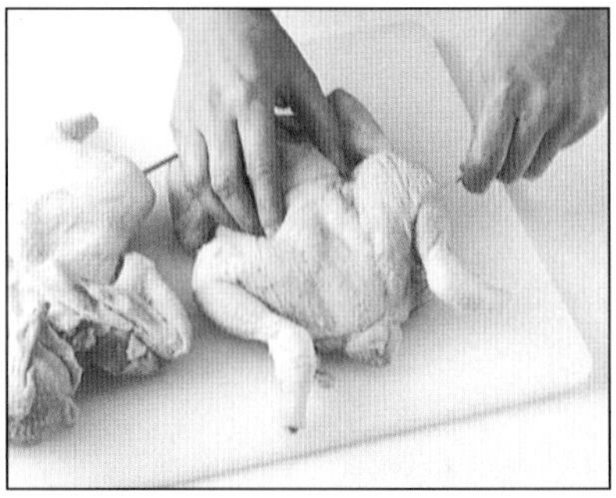

3 Open out a bird, skin side up, then press down firmly with the heel of your hand. Pass a long skewer through one leg and out through the other to secure the bird open and flat. Repeat with the remaining birds.

4 Spread the mustard mixture evenly over the skin of the birds. Cover loosely and put in a cool place for at least 2 hours. Preheat the broiler.

5 Place the birds, skin side up, under the broiler and cook for about 12 minutes. Turn over, baste and cook for another 7 minutes, until the juices run clear.

COOK'S TIP

Butterflied game hens cook well on the barbecue grill. Make sure the coals are hot, then cook for 15–20 minutes, turning and basting frequently.

Moroccan Chicken Couscous

A subtly spiced and fragrant dish with a fruity sauce.

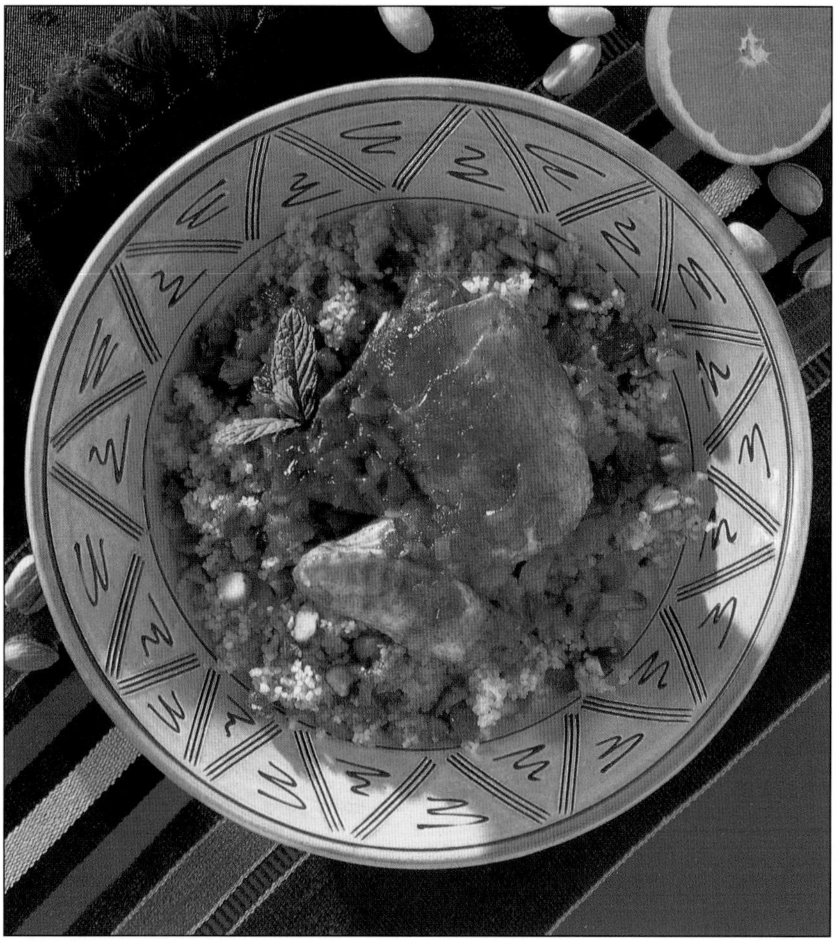

INGREDIENTS

Serves 4

1 tablespoon butter
1 tablespoon sunflower oil
4 chicken portions, about 6 ounces each
2 onions, finely chopped
2 garlic cloves, crushed
1/2 teaspoon ground cinnamon
1/4 teaspoon ground ginger
1/4 teaspoon ground turmeric
2 tablespoons orange juice
2 teaspoons honey
salt
fresh mint sprigs, to garnish

For the couscous

2 cups couscous
1 teaspoon salt
2 teaspoons sugar
2 tablespoons sunflower oil
1/2 teaspoon ground cinnamon
pinch of grated nutmeg
1 tablespoon orange flower water
2 tablespoons golden raisins
1/2 cup chopped blanched almonds
3 tablespoons chopped pistachios

1 Heat the butter and oil in a large pan and add the chicken portions, skin-side down. Fry for 3–4 minutes, until the skin is golden, then turn over.

2 Add the onions, garlic, spices and a pinch of salt and pour on the orange juice and 1 1/4 cups water. Cover and bring to a boil, then reduce the heat and simmer for about 30 minutes.

3 Meanwhile, place the couscous and salt in a bowl and cover with 1 1/2 cups water. Stir once and let stand for 5 minutes. Add the sugar, 1 tablespoon of the oil, the cinnamon, nutmeg, orange flower water and golden raisins and mix.

4 Heat the remaining 1 tablespoon oil in a pan and lightly fry the almonds until golden. Stir into the couscous with the pistachios.

5 Line a steamer with waxed paper and spoon in the couscous. Sit the steamer over the chicken (or over a pan of boiling water) and steam for 10 minutes.

6 Remove the steamer and keep covered. Stir the honey into the chicken liquid and boil rapidly for 3–4 minutes. Spoon the couscous onto a warmed serving platter. Top with the chicken, and some of the sauce. Garnish with the fresh mint and serve with the remaining sauce.

Spicy Masala Chicken

These chicken pieces are broiled and have a sweet-and-sour taste. They can be served cold with a salad and rice or hot with mashed potatoes.

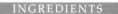

INGREDIENTS

Serves 6

12 chicken thighs
6 tablespoons lemon juice
1 teaspoon chopped fresh ginger
1 teaspoon chopped garlic
1 teaspoon crushed dried red chilies
1 teaspoon salt
1 teaspoon light brown sugar
2 tablespoons honey
2 tablespoons chopped fresh cilantro
1 green chili, finely chopped
2 tablespoons vegetable oil
fresh cilantro sprigs, to garnish

1 Prick the chicken thighs with a fork, rinse, pat dry and set aside in a bowl.

2 In a large mixing bowl, make the marinade by combining the lemon juice, ginger, garlic, crushed dried red chilies, salt, sugar and honey.

3 Transfer the chicken thighs to the spice mixture and coat well. Set aside for about 45 minutes.

4 Preheat the broiler to medium. Add the cilantro and chopped green chili to the chicken thighs and place them in a flameproof baking dish.

5 Pour any remaining marinade over the chicken and baste with the oil.

6 Broil the chicken thighs under the preheated broiler for 15–20 minutes, turning and basting occasionally, until they are cooked through and browned.

7 Transfer the chicken to a serving dish and garnish with a few sprigs of cilantro.

Quick Chicken Curry

Curry powder can be bought in three different strengths – mild, medium and hot. Use the type you prefer to suit your taste.

INGREDIENTS

Serves 4

8 chicken legs (thighs and drumsticks)
2 tablespoons vegetable oil
1 onion, thinly sliced
1 garlic clove, crushed
1 tablespoon curry powder
1 tablespoon all-purpose flour
1¾ cups homemade or canned chicken stock
1 beefsteak tomato
1 tablespoon mango chutney
1 tablespoon lemon juice
salt and black pepper

1 Cut the chicken legs in half. Heat the oil in a large flameproof casserole and brown the chicken pieces on all sides. Remove and keep warm.

2 Add the onion and crushed garlic to the casserole and cook until soft. Add the curry powder and cook gently for 2 minutes.

3 Add the flour, and gradually blend in the chicken stock and the seasoning.

4 Bring to a boil, replace the chicken pieces, cover and simmer for 20–30 minutes, or until tender and cooked through.

5 Blanch the tomato in boiling water for 45 seconds, then run it under cold water to loosen the skin. Peel and cut into small cubes.

6 Add to the chicken, with the mango chutney and lemon juice. Heat through gently and adjust the seasoning to taste.

Tandoori Chicken Kebabs

This dish originated on the plains of the Punjab at the foot of the Himalayas. There, food is traditionally cooked in clay ovens known as tandoors – hence the name.

INGREDIENTS

Serves 4

4 chicken breasts, about 6 ounces each, boned and skinned
1 tablespoon lemon juice
3 tablespoons tandoori paste, available at Indian stores and some supermarkets
3 tablespoons plain yogurt
1 garlic clove, crushed
2 tablespoons chopped cilantro
1 small onion, cut into wedges and separated into layers
a little oil, for brushing
salt and black pepper
cilantro sprigs, to garnish
pilaf rice and naan bread, to serve

1 Chop the chicken breasts into 1-inch cubes, place in a bowl and add the lemon juice, tandoori paste, yogurt, garlic, cilantro and seasoning. Cover and let marinate in the fridge for at least 2–3 hours.

2 Preheat the broiler. Thread alternate pieces of chicken and onion onto four skewers.

3 Brush the onions with a little oil, lay the kebabs on a broiler rack and cook under high heat for about 10–12 minutes, turning once. Garnish the kebabs with cilantro and serve at once with pilaf rice and naan bread.

Chinese Chicken with Cashew Nuts

A stir-fry of chicken with egg noodles, scallions and cashews.

INGREDIENTS

Serves 4

4 chicken breasts about 6 ounces each, boned, skinned and sliced into strips
3 garlic cloves, crushed
4 tablespoons soy sauce
2 tablespoons cornstarch
1 cup dried egg noodles
3 tablespoons peanut or sunflower oil
1 tablespoon sesame oil
1 cup roasted cashews
6 scallions, cut into 2-inch pieces and halved lengthwise
scallion curls and a little chopped red chili, to garnish

1 Put the chicken, garlic, soy sauce and cornstarch in a bowl and mix well. Cover and chill for about 30 minutes.

2 Bring a pan of water to a boil and add the noodles. Turn off the heat and let stand for 5 minutes. Drain well and reserve.

3 Heat the oils in a large frying pan and add the chicken and marinade. Stir-fry for about 3–4 minutes, or until golden brown.

4 Add the cashews and scallions to the pan and stir-fry for 2–3 minutes.

5 Add the drained noodles and stir-fry for another 2 minutes. Serve immediately, garnished with the scallion curls and chopped red chili.

Chicken with Spiced Rice

This is a good dish for entertaining. It can be prepared in advance and reheated in the oven. Serve with traditional curry accompaniments.

INGREDIENTS

Serves 8

2 pounds boneless chicken thighs
4 tablespoons olive oil
2 large onions, thinly sliced
1–2 green chilies, seeded and finely chopped
1 teaspoon grated fresh ginger
1 garlic clove, crushed
1 tablespoon hot curry powder
2/3 cup homemade or canned chicken stock
2/3 cup plain yogurt
2 tablespoons chopped fresh cilantro, to garnish
salt and black pepper

For the spiced rice

generous 2 1/4 cups white basmati rice
1/2 teaspoon garam masala
3 3/4 cups chicken stock or water
scant 1/2 cup dark or golden raisins
1/2 cup chopped toasted almonds

1 Put the basmati rice into a sieve and wash under cold running water to remove any starchy powder coating the grains. Then put into a bowl, cover with cold water and let soak for 30 minutes. The grains will absorb some water so that they will not stick together in a solid mass while cooking.

2 Preheat the oven to 325°F. Cut the chicken into bite-size cubes. Heat 2 tablespoons of the oil in a large flameproof casserole, add one onion and cook until softened. Add the finely chopped chilies, grated ginger, crushed garlic and curry powder to the casserole and continue cooking for another 2 minutes, stirring occasionally.

3 Add the stock and seasoning, and bring slowly to a boil. Add the chicken. Cover and bake for 20 minutes, or until tender.

4 Remove from the oven and stir in the yogurt.

5 Meanwhile, heat the remaining oil in a flameproof casserole and cook the remaining onion gently until tender and lightly browned. Add the drained rice, garam masala and stock or water. Bring to a boil, cover and cook in the oven with the chicken for 20–35 minutes, or until the rice is tender and all the stock has been absorbed.

6 To serve, stir the raisins and toasted almonds into the rice. Spoon half the rice into a large deep serving dish, cover with the chicken and then the remaining rice. Sprinkle with chopped cilantro to garnish.

Chicken Biryani

A deceptively easy curry to make, and very tasty, too.

INGREDIENTS

Serves 4

$1^1/_2$ cups basmati rice, rinsed
$^1/_2$ teaspoon salt
5 whole cardamom pods
2–3 whole cloves
1 cinnamon stick
3 tablespoons vegetable oil
3 onions, sliced
4 chicken breasts, 6 ounces each, cubed, skinned and boned
$^1/_4$ teaspoon ground cloves
5 cardamom pods, seeds removed and ground
$^1/_4$ teaspoon ground chilies
1 teaspoon ground cumin
1 teaspoon ground coriander
$^1/_2$ teaspoon black pepper
3 garlic cloves, finely chopped
1 teaspoon finely chopped fresh ginger
juice of 1 lemon
4 tomatoes, sliced
2 tablespoons chopped fresh cilantro
$^2/_3$ cup plain yogurt
$^1/_2$ teaspoon saffron strands soaked in 2 teaspoons hot milk
3 tablespoons toasted slivered almonds and fresh cilantro sprigs, to garnish
plain yogurt, to serve

1 Preheat the oven to 375°F. Bring a pan of water to a boil and add the rice, salt, cardamom pods, cloves and cinnamon stick. Boil for 2 minutes and then drain, leaving the whole spices in the rice.

2 Heat the oil in a pan and fry the onions for 8 minutes, until browned. Add the chicken followed by all the ground spices, the garlic, ginger and lemon juice. Stir-fry for 5 minutes.

3 Transfer the chicken mixture to a casserole and lay the sliced tomatoes on top. Sprinkle on the cilantro, spoon on the plain yogurt and top with the drained rice.

4 Drizzle the saffron and milk over the rice and pour on $^2/_3$ cup of water.

5 Cover tightly and bake in the oven for 1 hour. Transfer to a warmed serving platter and remove the whole spices from the rice. Garnish with toasted almonds and cilantro and serve with extra plain yogurt.

Chicken Naan Pockets

This quick and easy dish is ideal for a speedy snack, lunch or supper. To save time, use the ready-to-bake naans available in some supermarkets and Asian stores, or try warmed pita bread instead.

INGREDIENTS

Serves 4

- 4 ready-prepared naans
- 3 tablespoons plain low-fat yogurt
- $1^1/_2$ teaspoons garam masala
- 1 teaspoon ground chilies
- 1 teaspoon salt
- 3 tablespoons lemon juice
- 1 tablespoon chopped fresh cilantro
- 1 green chili, chopped
- $3^1/_4$ cups cubed chicken
- 1 tablespoon vegetable oil (optional)
- 8 onion rings
- 2 tomatoes, quartered
- $^1/_2$ white cabbage, shredded

To garnish

- lemon wedges
- 2 small tomatoes, halved
- mixed lettuce leaves
- fresh cilantro

1 Cut into the middle of each naan to make a pocket, then set aside.

2 Stir together the yogurt, garam masala, ground chilies, salt, lemon juice, fresh cilantro and chopped green chili. Pour the marinade over the chicken pieces and allow to marinate for about 1 hour.

3 Preheat the broiler to very hot, then lower the heat to medium. Place the chicken in a flameproof dish and broil for 15–20 minutes, until cooked, turning the chicken pieces at least twice.

4 Remove from the heat and fill each naan with the chicken, onion rings, tomatoes and cabbage. Serve with the garnish ingredients.

Chicken Tikka

This chicken dish is an extremely popular Indian appetizer and is quick and easy to cook. Chicken Tikka can also be served as a main course for four.

INGREDIENTS

Serves 6

- $3^1/_4$ cups cubed chicken
- 1 teaspoon chopped fresh ginger
- 1 teaspoon chopped garlic
- 1 teaspoon ground chilies
- $^1/_4$ teaspoon ground turmeric
- 1 teaspoon salt
- $^2/_3$ cup plain low-fat yogurt
- 4 tablespoons lemon juice
- 1 tablespoon chopped fresh cilantro
- 1 tablespoon vegetable oil

To garnish

- 1 small onion, cut into rings
- lime wedges
- mixed salad
- fresh cilantro

1 In a medium bowl, combine the chicken pieces, ginger, garlic, ground chilies, turmeric, salt, yogurt, lemon juice and fresh cilantro and marinate for at least 2 hours.

2 Place on a broiler pan or in a flameproof dish lined with foil and baste with the oil.

3 Preheat the broiler to medium. Broil the chicken for 15–20 minutes, until cooked, turning and basting two or three times. Serve with the garnish ingredients.

Sweet and Sour Kebabs

This marinade contains sugar and will burn very easily, so grill the kebabs slowly, turning often. It is delicious served with Harlequin Rice.

INGREDIENTS

Serves 4

2 chicken breasts, boned and skinned
8 pickling onions or 2 medium onions
4 strips rindless lean bacon
3 firm bananas
1 red bell pepper, seeded and sliced

For the marinade

2 tablespoons light brown sugar
1 tablespoon Worcestershire sauce
2 tablespoons lemon juice
salt and black pepper

For the Harlequin Rice

2 tablespoons olive oil
generous 1 cup cooked rice
1 cup cooked peas
1 small red bell pepper, seeded and diced

1 Mix together the marinade ingredients. Cut each chicken breast into four pieces, add to the marinade, cover and leave for at least 4 hours or preferably overnight in the fridge.

2 Peel the pickling onions, blanch them in boiling water for 5 minutes and drain. If using medium onions, quarter them after blanching.

3 Cut each strip of bacon in half. Peel the bananas and cut each into three pieces. Wrap a strip of bacon around each piece of banana.

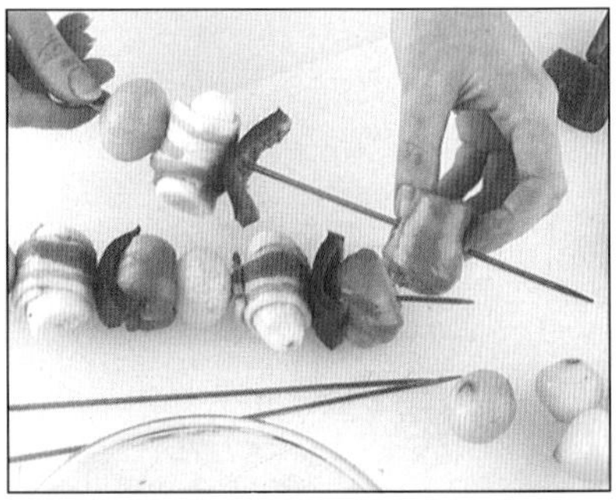

4 Thread onto metal skewers with the chicken pieces, onions and pepper slices. Brush with the marinade.

5 Broil or grill over low coals for 15 minutes, turning and basting frequently with the marinade. Keep warm while you prepare the rice.

6 Heat the oil in a frying pan and add the rice, peas and diced pepper. Stir until heated through and serve with the kebabs.

Chinese Chicken Wings

These are best eaten with fingers as an appetizer. Make sure you provide finger bowls and plenty of paper napkins; things could get messy.

INGREDIENTS

Serves 4

12 chicken wings
3 garlic cloves, crushed
$1^1/_2$-inch piece fresh ginger, grated
juice of 1 large lemon
3 tablespoons soy sauce
3 tablespoons honey
$^1/_2$ teaspoon ground chilies
$^2/_3$ cup chicken stock
salt and black pepper
lemon wedges, to garnish

1 Remove the wing tips and use to make the stock. Cut the wings into two pieces.

2 Combine the remaining ingredients, except for the stock, and coat the chicken pieces in the mixture. Cover with plastic wrap and marinate overnight.

3 Preheat the oven to 425°F. Remove the wings from the marinade and arrange in a single layer in a roasting pan. Bake for 20–25 minutes, basting at least twice with the marinade during cooking.

4 Place the wings on a serving plate. Add the stock to the marinade in the roasting pan, and bring to a boil. Cook to a syrupy consistency and spoon a little over the wings. Serve garnished with lemon wedges.

Index

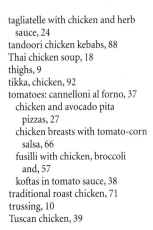